# ACNE

**Ronald Marks** is Professor of Dermatology at the Welsh National School of Medicine in Cardiff. He has lectured extensively, and is the author of *Psoriasis*, also in this series. He has written and edited several medical textbooks, including *Practical Problems in Dermatology, Common Facial Dermatoses* and *Investigative Techniques in Dermatology*.

Prof Marks is Chairman of the International Society for Bioengineering and the Skin and a Past President of the European Society for Dermatological Research. His hobbies are art appreciation and playing squash.

POSITIVE HEALTH GUIDE

# ACNE
## Advice on clearing
## your skin

### Prof Ronald Marks,
### FRCP, MRCPath

## MARTIN DUNITZ

To Hilary and my two spotty daughters

© **Ronald Marks 1984**
First published in the United Kingdom in 1984
by Martin Dunitz Ltd, London

Reprinted 1985

**British Library Cataloguing in Publication Data**

Marks, Ronald
    Acne.(Positive health guide)
    I. Acne.
    I. Title. II. Series.
    616.5'3 RL131
    ISBN 0-906348-53-6
    ISBN 0-906348-52-8 (pbk)


Phototypeset in Garamond by Input Typesetting Ltd, London
Printed by Toppan Printing Company (s) Pte Ltd, Singapore

# CONTENTS

# INTRODUCTION

## Acne – facts and fancy

Not many of us are lucky enough to escape some spots during the teenage years. In fact, it is estimated that 70 per cent of the teenage population at any one time has a recognizable degree of acne, and it is so common that some doctors believe it is a normal part of growing up and not a disease at all. It is true that not everyone has easily visible acne and that only a minority have bad enough acne to want to consult a doctor, but probably everyone at some time has at least the beginnings of acne. In my experience of seeing and treating patients with acne in Britain, other countries of Europe, and the USA, I have found people have plenty of questions that need answering. In this book I shall describe the way that we think acne develops. You will see that dermatologists have spent a lot of time investigating the condition, but there is still a lot to be learnt.

Although acne is familiar to most of us, its causes and remedies are still surrounded by myth and folklore, and it is common to hear such questions as 'Is it due to something in my diet, doctor?' I shall show how having acne has nothing to do with what you eat; neither can you catch it! The number of articles in magazines on the subject of teenage spots shows how interested many people are, and I believe this indicates that a book such as this is needed to put straight outdated ideas and give all you need to know about acne: the causes, the different types, the remedies you can try yourself and those that your doctor may prescribe.

There are large numbers of creams, lotions, and medicated cosmetics for treating acne on sale across the counter. There are also medicated soaps, and shampoos, as well as pills of various types, and sunlamps. Are any of these self treatments effective? Do they have any dangers? I have tried to answer these questions as fully as possible. You may well never need to go to your doctor, but will want information and advice about what to buy.

Sympathy is not the most noticeable reaction to people with acne, although it can cause quite a lot of misery and discomfort. So I hope too in this book to give some help and reassurance by explaining how to deal with your own skin problem and the unhappiness it causes, and with other people's attitudes to you.

Although the book is primarily intended for those with acne who want to know what is going on in their skin and how to cope with the problem,

7

I believe that it should also be read by families and friends of people with acne. General practitioners, nurses and others concerned with health care should also find it useful.

In Chapter 1 I shall be dealing with how acne develops, after which I suggest various ways in which you can clear up mild attacks yourself. The more serious forms and how doctors treat them I describe in Chapters 5 and 6. You can use this as a handbook and read only the chapters which deal with your particular condition; but it is a good idea for everyone to look at the first chapter for the basic information about the skin and the way it changes in acne.

# 1 WHAT IS ACNE?

Acne is a skin disease that we still need to research; as you will see in this chapter, the causes are even now not fully understood. Yet we have developed treatments that will in time help even the worst of conditions. In Stephen's case we were able to find the root of the problem and treat his acne successfully by giving him the right lotion and changing his duties for a short time:

Stephen, an eighteen-year-old in the army, had had a few spots on his face for about nine months. He put it down to his corporal 'getting at him'. Suddenly, a few weeks before I saw him, he developed a serious acne condition over his back. He said this was due to getting very hot during a long route march – and he may have been right! Stephen's back improved quite quickly after his having some medical treatment and being changed to light duties only, and after three months it was clear of spots. By that time he was no longer suffering from spots on his face.

The make-up of normal skin.

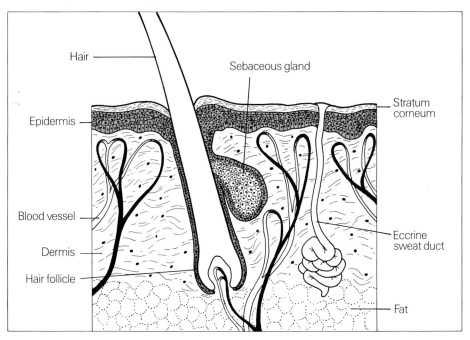

# Normal skin

To understand what is going on in the skin in acne you need to know something of the way skin works and how it is put together, so to start I will describe briefly how normal skin is made up.

**The layers** It has three layers: a tough, outer horny part called the stratum corneum, the epidermis and the dermis. Beneath these is a layer of subcutaneous fat separating the muscles from the skin (see page 9).

**The pores** If you take a magnifying glass and look at a patch of skin you will see pores (small holes) in the skin surface, some with hairs projecting from them, others without. The pits that don't have hairs are sweat pores – the openings of the sweat glands. Those with hairs are the hair follicles. Both the hairs and the sweat glands are formed by the epidermis but they penetrate the epidermis and have their 'roots' in the dermis (see above).

**The colour** depends on the blood in the skin and the colour of the skin itself, which is made by a black pigment (colouring) called melanin. This is produced by special cells called melanocytes which are situated in the bottom part of the epidermis. Everyone has the same number of melanocytes whatever the colour of skin, but the darker a person's skin is, the harder the pigment cells are working to produce pigment.

### The epidermis and horny layer
It is worthwhile describing the epidermis and its horny layer in more detail as they are important in acne. The epidermis is made up of various types of cells and forms the visible top layers of the skin without blood vessels.

**The stratum corneum** is the tough outer layer, not like a protective coat in the normal sense as it is constantly being renewed. Cells from the epidermis are always being produced and slowly moving upwards to the horny layer. It takes, on average, about twenty-eight days for an epidermal cell to travel from the base of the epidermis to become a horn cell at the top of the epidermis and then be shed at the surface of the horny layer. The process of the older horn cells dropping off as new ones are made is called desquamation. On most parts of the skin the horny layer is very thin: while the usual thickness of the epidermis is around 0.05 mm, the stratum corneum is only 0.015 mm. It never ceases to amaze me that such an important and protective part of the skin is so thin. On the palms and soles of the feet the horny layer is, not surprisingly, much thicker – about 0.5 mm.

**Hair follicles** Hairs are produced in pits in the skin called hair follicles. As mentioned above, the hairs are made from epidermis, even though the follicles reach down far into tough dermis. It is as though you had stuck your finger through a sheet of Plasticine and made a narrow channel of Plasticine around it. The hair is produced by very special epidermal cells at the bottom of the pit called hair matrix cells but the walls of the pit still produce horn in the same way as they do on the skin's surface. It is this horn in the hair follicle that forms the blackhead or comedone (see page 13).

**Sebaceous glands** Each hair follicle has an oil gland attached to it called the sebaceous gland. This delivers sebum, an oily mixture of different types of fat, into the follicle, from where it drains to the surface along the hair. Sebum is made by the sebaceous gland cells. They collect globules of fat inside themselves and eventually they break down into an oily sludge. No one is quite sure about the function of sebum, although some believe that it serves to lubricate the hair.

One important type of fat in sebum is known as triglyceride and is similar to the fat found in meat. The bacteria that live in the skin are in the hair follicles and as sebum moves towards the skin surface the triglycerides are split into other substances by the action of the bacteria. These substances include fatty acids that can be irritating, and may well be important in causing acne.

The composition of sebum is quite similar in people of all types and it doesn't vary much according to their diet. However, the rate of sebum secretion (at which sebum is made) does. This explains why some people have greasy skins and some do not. People with acne tend to have a higher rate of sebum secretion than those without acne. And people who have bad acne are likely to secrete much more sebum than those who have only mild acne.

The sebaceous glands vary greatly in size. Those in the acne areas – the face, back and chest – are very large compared to those in other areas. Interestingly enough, the hairs in these follicles with large sebaceous glands tend to be quite small and insignificant – a fact that may be of great importance in acne. Large hairs keep the hair follicles open, allowing the sebum to drain away, whereas the small hairs permit blackheads to form (see page 13).

## The dermis
The tough dermis is made up of fibres called collagen and elastin that give the skin strength and elasticity and it contains the blood vessels and nerves of the skin. They reach right up to the base of the epidermis but don't actually penetrate it. When people with acne get inflamed skin, most of the changes take place in the dermis, including scarring, so this area is also important in acne.

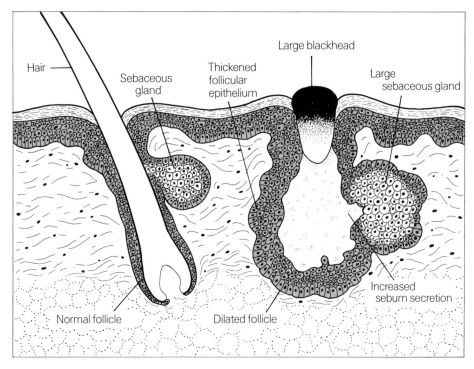

Hair

Sebaceous gland

Thickened follicular epithelium

Large blackhead

Large sebaceous gland

Normal follicle

Dilated follicle

Increased sebum secretion

Blackheads are formed in hair follicles.

# How does acne start?

When acne occurs, a number of changes take place in these different parts of the skin which result in the blackheads and spots forming. How this happens is quite complicated. First I shall discuss the visible signs of acne.

### Where does it appear?

You can get acne anywhere you have hairs because it is in the hair follicles that it starts. However, it is only hair follicles where there are large sebaceous glands that are usually affected and these are on your face, back, shoulders and chest. For this reason it is the face, shoulders, back and chest that are most commonly affected. You are unlikely to have many other places affected if your acne is mild and with only slight inflammation. But if you have a fairly severe outbreak you may also have acne spots on the back of your neck, upper arms, buttocks or thighs. Usually the number of areas of skin affected is a good measure of the severity of a case.

## What are the causes and what does it look like?

Acne is such a common skin disorder that nearly everyone can recognize it when they see it. But there are spots that only look like acne and really are due to something else; and sometimes acne spots can take on a quite different appearance and then it needs a practised eye to recognize them. I shall describe these unusual types in Chapter 6. Here I explain the common features of acne. The most important are:

1. The blackhead (comedone or comedo)
2. Increased oiliness of the skin, called seborrhoea
3. Inflamed spots (papules) and pus spots (pustules).

## Blackheads

Blackheads are found in some areas of your skin more than in others. They are most common on the face, chest and back – just the places where acne spots are found; although many people have blackheads in these areas without the other features of acne. With acne you nearly always get some blackheads on your face, though sometimes they can be difficult to see. They occur most frequently on and around the nose, on the forehead,

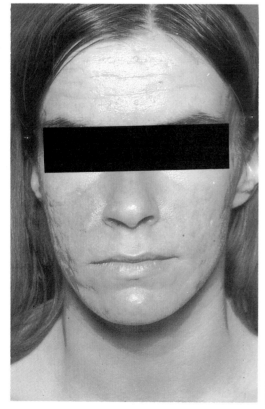

People with acne usually have a greasy skin condition called seborrhoea.

around the ears and on the chin. Although you can get rid of them by pressing hard on either side of their tips, some don't leave their burrows without a struggle! I will talk about whether it is a good thing or not to remove them later (Chapter 3).

If the horn cells from the hair follicles of someone with acne are looked at very closely indeed, with a special, powerful microscope known as the electron microscope, fat droplets can be seen inside the cells. As these droplets are not usually found in horn cells and therefore indicate abnormal horn formation, they may be a clue to what is causing the blackheads.

The formation of blackheads, or comedones, is an early and important development in acne. Somehow the horn in the hair follicle becomes stickier. The horn cells do not separate one from the other very easily but tend to stay bound together, and so clog the follicle (see diagram on page 12). Researchers are trying hard to understand the reason for this increase in stickiness. When they have cracked this problem we will be much nearer to designing more effective treatments!

The top of the comedone is black – which of course is why it is known as a blackhead. The story of the various explanations for the dark tip of a blackhead is quite amusing. Before anyone had looked at skin down a microscope it was commonly believed that blackheads were tiny worms or grubs and that the black bit was the head of the worm. Later on, in the age when 'cleanliness was next to godliness' and dirt was blamed for anything bad, the blackhead tips were thought to be ingrained dirt. Acne itself was supposed to occur in people who didn't wash their faces! A more recent explanation for the black bits was that the fats in the comedone were oxidized (changed chemically) at the skin surface by the oxygen in the atmosphere and changed to a black colour. Now we know that all these suggestions were wrong. It has been found that the black colour is ordinary skin pigment, that is, melanin. The reason for the pigment being at the tip is that pigment producing cells called melanocytes are situated along the bottom part of the epidermis and around the upper part of the hair follicle canal, but not in the lower part. This means the horn cells produced in the upper part of the hair follicle will be darkly pigmented but that the horn cells lower down will not – and it is the upper horn cells that clog the follicle at the surface. It is as simple as that!

Not only the hair follicles but all the skin may be affected by this curious stickiness of the follicular horn cells. The horn of the skin around the hair follicles is thicker than normal and may not fall off as readily at the surface. You may notice you have slightly scaly skin in these places.

### Whiteheads

So far I have talked about ordinary blackheads that are easily recognized when you look at the skin. Of more importance are the ones that you cannot see. Very small blackheads which require a powerful magnifying glass to be seen are always present when there are easily visible big ones.

The tips of these small ones may not be black at all and they are sometimes called whiteheads. They are also horny plugs in hair follicles but these follicles are very much smaller than the ones with blackheads. It seems likely that some of these whiteheads become the papules or inflamed spots of acne (see page 17).

## Changes in the hair follicle itself

The hair follicle canal with a blackhead in it becomes irregular and thickened at first. Later on other changes occur. One curious thing that defies explanation at present concerns the sebaceous glands in follicles with blackheads. The glands wither and shrink – odd, as you will see (below) that overall there is *increased* sebum secretion in acne. Perhaps the sebaceous glands disappear only in a few follicles, leaving the others to produce the sebum.

## Greasy skin or seborrhoea

This is the name for the greasy, shiny complexion of people with acne and it is due to the increased rate of production of sebum by the sebaceous glands of the hair follicles. As with blackheads, it is quite common to have

Acne spots (*left*) and cysts (*right*) start in the inflamed dermis.

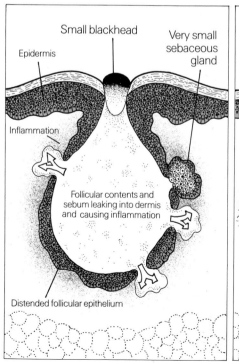
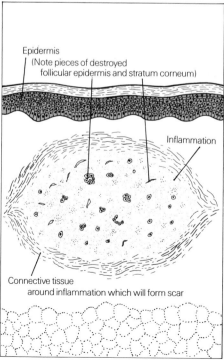

seborrhoea without acne, but uncommon to have acne with no seborrhoea. Usually the more the seborrhoea the worse is the acne.

**What causes seborrhoea?** Hormones play a large part. They are chemical messengers produced by glands and circulating in the blood. The sebaceous glands are controlled by the male sex hormones called androgens. The main androgen is called testosterone. Both sexes have testosterone in their blood but men have four or five times more than women. In men most of the testosterone is produced in the testicles but some is produced in important glands that rest on top of the kidneys known as suprarenal glands or adrenal glands. In women most of the testosterone is produced in the adrenal glands but some seems to be produced in the ovaries as well. The levels of testosterone in the blood of children is very low and it goes up at the time of puberty in both sexes. The size of the sebaceous glands also changes at the time of puberty, increasing to adult proportions. As you may expect, the rate of sebum secretion increases as well.

Girl acne sufferers may, it seems, have slightly increased levels of androgens in their blood, while eunuchs have very little testosterone. They don't secrete much sebum and, very interestingly, they don't suffer from acne. If they are given treatment with testosterone their sebaceous glands enlarge and they start to secrete more sebum. When they secrete more sebum they can start to develop acne!

**Open pores**
This is an accompanying feature to acne, although open pores are not part of the skin changes in the disease. You are likely to get open pores or what is often described as 'orange peel' skin in the acne areas because of the seborrhoea and other changes in the hair follicles, which cause the pores to open up. This feature is no more permanent than the other aspects of acne.

**Bacteria**
There are two main types of bacteria that live on the skin and a yeast type of fungus. They are all over the skin surface but are most numerous in hair follicles. These unseen and silent minute foreigners on the skin surface do not normally cause any harm – and may even do some good. Tiny mites also live in the sebaceous follicles of the face and these are also quite benign passengers.

In acne there seems to be an increase in the numbers of bacteria present. The reason why they multiply has not yet been discovered. However, some very sophisticated research studies show that the bacteria on the skin of people with acne may differ in subtle ways from those on people with normal skin – particularly in the way the bacteria split the triglycerides in the hair follicles into fatty acids. If this is confirmed it could be important in finding new treatments.

The two types of bacteria on normal and acne type skin are called staphylococcus epidermidis and proprionebacterium acnes; most acne researchers have concentrated on the second. One interesting point about these bacteria is that they thrive best in an atmosphere that is very low in oxygen, and are known as anaerobic. The follicle blocked by a blackhead probably provides an atmosphere with little oxygen, which allows the bacteria to grow happily, splitting the triglycerides into fatty acids.

**Are acne bacteria infectious?** Although we don't know all the details of the way the bacteria are involved in acne we are pretty certain about one point. That is, they are not infecting the skin in the same way that other bacteria do, for example, when they cause a boil (see page 85), impetigo or an infected cut. You can't catch acne – if you could, all dermatologists (skin specialists) would have it all the time!

### Inflammation

One of the most noticeable signs of acne is red, inflamed skin. Like seborrhoea, this is linked to the number of blackheads in your skin. Hair follicles blocked with blackheads split or crack, so that their contents contact the sensitive dermis. This means that sebum, horn cells, and bacteria leak into the dermis through the cracks in the wall of the follicle. We think that this is the main cause of the inflammation in acne.

When there is inflammation, the minute blood vessels of the skin become wider and the blood flows faster in them. This is why your skin looks redder than usual and is warm to the touch. Fluid leaks out of these wide blood vessels into the tissues of the dermis, making them swell up. White blood cells also find their way out of the blood vessels and accumulate inside and around the affected hair follicle. As the inflammation in the dermis worsens so the acne papules are formed. When white cells collect inside the damaged hair follicle a pustule develops. The follicle with a comedone has been described as a time bomb. The explosion is the bacteria and horn of the follicle canal escaping into the exposed and sensitive dermis. If the explosion is only a mild one then a small papule develops.

**Papules** are red and either steeple-shaped or their tips are more gently rounded. The papules usually last only a few days and when they subside they leave no trace. The few that stay on the skin for a long time tend to become hard to the touch and a duller red in colour. These also leave no trace when they do go, but they may be visible and detectable to the touch for some weeks and even months after the obvious inflammation has gone.

**Pustules** These develop either at the tip of papules, where pus can gather (and are then known as papulopustules) and later discharge, or they occur by themselves, alongside the papulopustules. Pustules which develop by

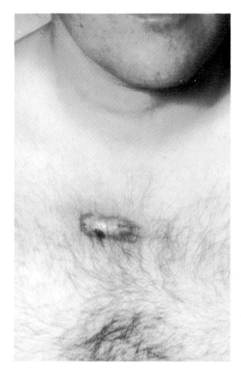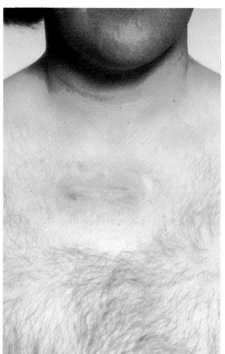

Even keloid scars can be healed with proper treatment.

themselves last only a day or two before their pus discharges and a small crust forms on the surface.

**Cysts** These happen when the explosion, described above, is a big one. Then some of the normal dermis is destroyed and vast numbers of white blood cells collect. The dermis in this area tries to protect itself by building a wall of scar-type tissue around the inflamed area. This is the basis of an acne cyst. Although it is always called a cyst the term is not really appropriate because in medicine a cyst usually means a collection of fluid inside a cavity or 'sac' lined by a type of skin. Acne cysts aren't like this at all; they consist of a softish part of pus (white blood cells) at the centre surrounded by a type of scar tissue.

Cysts are usually several times larger than the ordinary papules and are often very painful and sore to the touch. The cysts can occur anywhere on the skin where other acne spots are found but are most common on the back of the neck, on the shoulders, on the line of the lower jaw and on the front of the chest. Some of the cysts become very red and inflamed, others are much less angry. Some burst and discharge their contents, others remain unchanged for weeks on end. Eventually they disappear, but they are more likely to leave scars than most other acne spots and blemishes.

18

## Scarring – is it permanent?

After all the inflammation that I have just described quietens down, the skin tries to repair the damage. This often results in scarring. No one really knows what controls the development of a scar, but the degree of damage needed to release the trigger varies tremendously in different people at different ages. Both sexes between fifteen and twenty are particularly likely to get large scars, even after relatively mild acne. The scars are of several types:

**Pock scars** When a hair follicle becomes affected and inflamed it may not regain its original shape and size easily after the redness and swelling have disappeared. It then takes on the appearance of a small pit. Sometimes the pits expand to produce a broad, round shallow depression in the skin (a pock scar, similar to the sort people have after chickenpox). Sometimes the scars are sunken but have a triangular shape.

**Hypertrophic scars** When large papules and cysts begin to clear up a hard, raised lump stays behind. For reasons that are not well understood, some of these lumps grow to become hypertrophic scars. They are pink, dome shaped and hard to the touch. Generally, they subside after a few months.

**Keloid scars** Occasionally the scar becomes aggressive, continuing to enlarge until it is much bigger than the original spot and seems to develop extensions into the surrounding normal skin. This result of inflammation is known as a keloid scar, and often seems to be caused by an acne cyst. Keloid scars mostly occur on the front of the chest and over the shoulders.

Whatever type of scarring you get in acne, it will eventually improve by itself. Of course the more serious the scars, the longer this will take. Bad keloid scars, for example, can last into middle or old age, but even they will very gradually be getting better as time goes by. Even while it is prominent, don't forget in the long term people value you much more for yourself – for your personality and your merits – than for your looks, so try not to worry too much if you get scars. I shall have more to say about this in Chapter 4.

When scarring is very marked, however, it is possible to improve it with drug treatments. I would recommend this for anyone who is especially upset by having heavy, visible scarring; though I think plastic surgery is not often a good idea as it may involve quite serious surgery and if unsuccessful would be doubly distressing.

Russell was nineteen when he started worrying about his acne scars staying with him for life. He was rather self-conscious about his spots and he had had acne for about three years before he tried to get some help. It wasn't all that severe but every so often he came out in a crop of quite large and tender spots. Antibiotic tablets prescribed by his doctor didn't seem to control it at first, until it was realized that he took the tablets irregularly – missing some days out altogether. Unfortunately, by the time he started proper treatment some damage had already been done to his skin. He had quite a few pitted scars over his cheeks and forehead and one or two larger, prominent scars over his shoulders and the back of his neck. These large, hypertrophic scars were treated by a dermatologist with injections of a strong corticosteroid (see page 62), which improved them considerably. Russell asked about plastic surgery for his other scars but was told that he didn't need it as the scars would become much less prominent within a few months now that his acne was under control, and that the scars were not as bad as he thought anyway.

### Redness
Sometimes the damage to the skin caused by the acne process results in injured small blood vessels. These blood vessels become wider than usual and make the skin of the affected part redder than normal. This is why some people have persistent redness of the cheeks, nose and chin. The redness and background of injury to the dermis can, rarely, lead on to the separate condition called rosacea (see page 82).

### Patterns of acne
I have described the various events in acne separately but of course they are all going on in the skin at the same time. If you were to look at the skin of someone with acne down a microscope you would see that all these stages were happening somewhere in the affected areas. However, each of the spots and scars follows the same pattern – or life cycle – as it develops. This can change at different times, but mostly it stays the same in any one person.

# What are the common types of acne?

### Mild acne
This is the commonest sort of acne; in fact most of us have it at some time and to some degree during our teens – which is why the condition is often called teenage spots. You usually see lots of little papules, pustules and blackheads on a background of greasy skin. The forehead, chin and lower jaw are the usual places for these to appear. You may also get spots scattered elsewhere in the acne areas (see page 12) but generally the face is mainly affected. This type of acne does not often continue for long without a break. It may last for a few months at a time or come in shorter waves with a few quiet weeks in between attacks of spots. Most people have just

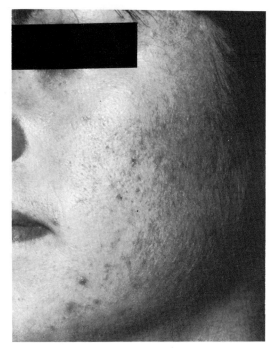

Mild acne is very common and hardly noticeable.

a few acne spots at any one time and often do not want to bother with medical treatment.

It does not follow that if you get mild acne, you will develop any of the severer types later and this mild acne does not cause much discomfort or interfere with work. Scarring is not common. Only a few pits may remain when the spots have gone.

## Moderate acne

About 10 per cent of all people with acne have this quite common type. There are more papules than in the superficial type of acne and they tend to be larger. Sometimes the papules develop into papulopustules (see page 17) but the pus spots may also occur by themselves. Usually more than one acne area is involved and spots often occur over the shoulders and on the chest. Some of the spots may be quite sore and tender for a time, with single spots coming and going. As with most types of acne, it tends to be worse in the winter time and to clear a bit in the summer (mainly due to climate and perhaps lighter clothing).

Generally this type of acne improves in the late teens or early twenties, although it can continue for some years more. Occasionally people get papulopustular acne for the first time in their twenties or thirties or, rarely, even later. I have seen people who have suddenly experienced this type of acne for the first time in their fifties or sixties, but this is really quite uncommon.

21

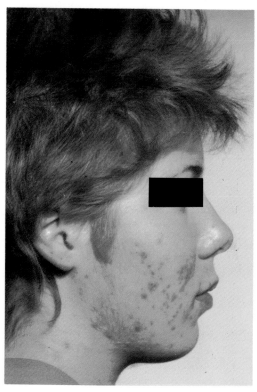

Moderate acne with typical acne spots.

Usually it doesn't leave much in the way of scars. A few acne pits may be left, but if the spots are not squeezed or picked then generally this type of acne leaves the skin looking quite healthy.

### Severe acne

A small proportion of people with acne have this type (2 or 3 per cent of all acne patients). The only real difference between this and moderate acne is that there is more and it is more persistent. There are large numbers of big spots on all the acne areas, and the spots tend to overflow on to other areas such as the middle or even the lower back or the upper arms. Individual spots may become quite large and very tender and cause a great deal of discomfort. Young men are more often affected by this more severe type of acne than women, and it can be quite a problem for young men in the uniformed services (because of their heavy physical duties involving sweating). As with milder types, the spots improve in the summer, but not always to the same extent. The amount of scarring that the condition leaves need not be very great. It depends on the treatment and on the amount of picking, squeezing and scratching that takes place. Mostly, very few scars remain after the condition subsides and those that do improve gradually over the years that follow.

## Picker's acne

Doctors are sometimes consulted by young women about spots on their faces which seem quite unnoticeable to everyone but themselves. When the spots are examined closely they look a little different to the usual acne pimples. The central part of the spot is not like the top of a tiny mountain but is covered by a scab or looks raw. This is because the spot has been scratched or picked (we call it excoriated). It is quite common for all the spots to be picked. We all have a compulsive urge to scratch, pick and squeeze all types of spots and blemishes on the skin. Virtually everyone with acne has picked at or otherwise interfered with some of their spots before they are seen by their doctor. I shall talk about this more in Chapter 3. But the group of girls that I am describing here are different. They have very little real acne but many small, picked pimples. The French have a marvellous descriptive name for the condition: *acne excoriée des jeunes filles* – excoriated acne of young women. Curiously enough, it is quite uncommon in young men.

Often girls with picker's acne are obsessed by the effect that the condition has on their appearance. Despite the fact that there may be very little real acne to be seen, they will not be reassured. Unfortunately the mauling that they give their skin can result in scars, so that their efforts to clear the spots are counter-productive, to say the least!

It is not difficult to see how the habit grows if acne spots keep coming back just when you are feeling low.

Severe acne can be cleared up as successfully as mild cases. This girl was treated with minocycline (see Chapter 5).

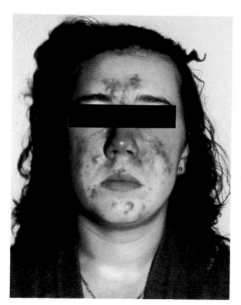 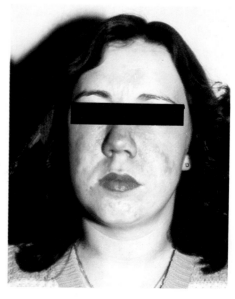

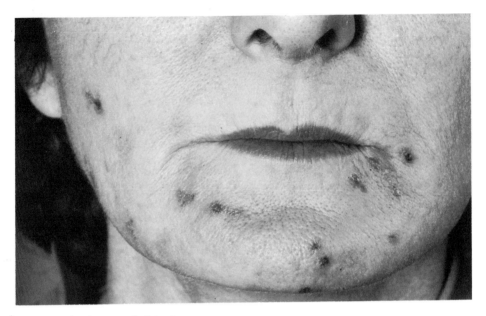

The scratched spots of picker's acne.

Rachel was a postgraduate student. She had done well so far but had worked terribly hard to keep near the top. She had had spots off and on since she was sixteen, but they were not too troublesome until her early twenties, when a few more appeared. She had always been a bit of a picker and when she got more spots she fiddled and picked harder. Instead of removing the spots it seemed to make them more prominent! She tried many of the recommended creams and lotions from her local pharmacy but nothing seemed to help.

Eventually she went to her doctor, who sent her to the dermatology clinic at her local hospital. When the skin specialist looked closely at her skin he couldn't see any undisturbed spots. Every one showed the effects of squeezing and picking. Some that had recently been scratched had scabs on, others that had been fiddled with a few weeks earlier were either red blemishes or little pits in the skin surface.

Not only was Rachel's skin in a bit of a mess but she was in quite a nervous state as well. She was weepy and depressed about her spots and life in general. The dermatologist had a long chat with her, explaining that a lot of trouble was due to overwork and tension and that her blemishes were mostly the result of her own busy fingers. He gave her a cream containing benzoyl peroxide (see page 57) and wrote to her doctor advising that he should see her for a series of chats. Rachel improved considerably and finished off her thesis – to the relief of all around her. She is still a bit of a picker but now has fewer spots to pick and is much less anxious and tense since the stress has been relieved.

When I have talked to girls with picker's acne, they have usually been quite anxious and depressed. They seem to focus their anxiety and depression on to the acne, but their nervous problem often stems from a variety of other sources. My experience is that many girls with this affliction need some type of sympathetic counselling.

## Cosmetic and fringe (bang) acne
This is mostly due to excessive oil and grease, which clog up the hair follicles. Many cosmetic products contain heavy oils which can cause acne in this way.

One fairly common example of this is a type of acne that has been called fringe acne, or bang acne in North America. It is so-called because it occurs under a fringe or bang that covers the forehead. It has been suggested that, as well as grease coming from the hair, oily hair dressings are responsible for the spots.

Although many of these descriptions may sound unpleasant, they are the body's usual response to minor injury caused in the dermis (lowest layer of the skin) by blackheads blocking the hair follicles. All of us have a small degree of inflammation at some point in our body most of the time. It would be wrong to think of acne as some very special, different type of reaction. The reason that it becomes a distressing, painful annoyance is because quite a lot of inflammation occurs at the same time in an easily visible area of skin. In the next chapter I try to explain why some people are more likely to get acne than others and what conditions seem to make it worse.

Acne most commonly affects teenagers and young adults.

# 2 WHO GETS ACNE?

In this chapter I shall talk about which types of people seem to suffer most and how everyday situations can affect your acne – first those that are known to influence acne, then the conditions which seem to make acne worse in some people, although we certainly don't know all the reasons for this. Finally I will discuss the absolute myths that have sprung up about acne.

## Conditions affecting everyone with acne

### Which age group is most affected?
Everyone knows that acne predominantly affects teenagers and usually lasts until the early twenties. In fact, in the few surveys that have been done of schoolchildren and young soldiers, acne of some degree has been found in

Working with oily machinery can cause acne.

about 70 per cent. More rarely, it can start in boys and girls of about nine or ten and last in adults as late as the thirties or even early forties. It also occurs, very infrequently, in infancy and old age (see Chapter 6).

## Do boys or girls suffer more?

There is general agreement that boys get acne more severely than girls – although of course some young women also have unpleasant outbreaks. It is not surprising that boys are greater sufferers when you consider the relationship of male sex hormones to acne (see page 16).

The relative numbers of boys and girls with acne have never been assessed, but, for the same reason that boys get worse acne, more of them in total are likely to have it to some visible degree in the teenage years.

## Which groups of people get acne?

Although there are many diseases that some racial groups get more than others, this is not the case with acne. As far as we know, all racial types get acne. However, it is thought that the severer forms of acne are more common in some groups than in others. White-skinned Caucasians seem to get it most severely. People from India living in Western countries can also be quite badly affected, as can black Africans in Europe and North America, but whether they are in their home countries we do not yet know. It seems that acne is less severe in Japanese and Chinese types, but once again, we do not have accurate information. I have heard it said that Eskimos, who are of the same racial type, have very little acne.

## Does your environment affect your chances of having acne?

Since acne is so common in North America, Australia and Europe, there is a suspicion (and certainly no more than a suspicion) that this reflects the overall wealth of the community. In my own experience the severer varieties of acne are much more common in North America than in the United Kingdom or the rest of Europe. Since in America there are all racial types, it seems that environment or social practices are more important than race.

Climate plays a small role too. Sunlight helps clear some people's acne (see Chapter 3), although it doesn't stop anyone living in a sunny area from developing it. Moving to a different climate does have one effect – if you already have acne and move to a hot, humid zone, the acne may become much worse due to excessive sweating (see page 75).

## Your job

**Can it cause acne?** Jobs in which you are exposed to oils and grease (for example, as a machine minder or motor mechanic) can cause acne because the oil irritates the hair follicles (see page 16). If you begin to get acne after starting a job of this sort, you should arrange that contact with the oil is eliminated, or at least very much reduced. A severer form of acne can be

Wearing heavy or tight clothes will be uncomfortable and may make your acne worse.

caused by working with chemical substances. I shall describe this in more detail in Chapter 6. These are examples of what is called occupational acne. Another is due to continuous irritation of an acne area. For instance, acne can develop on the side of a violin player's neck, where the rest touches the skin.

**Will it make acne worse?** Some jobs tend to make acne worse rather than actually cause it. For example, boiler stokers and bakers tend to get very hot while they work. They sweat, their hair follicle pores become blocked by the sweating and this can make acne worse. The same is true of any hot, energetic job which is dirty and causes sweating. Presumably this is the reason why some soldiers in the tropical zones have developed very bad acne. However, in nearly all cases attacks like this can be cleared up with the proper treatment. Only if no improvement can be made while you work in high temperatures should you consider changing your job.

David erupted in several large and tender papules over his face, neck and back in the space of two or three weeks. He was nineteen and an apprentice baker, and at first he paid no attention to the inflamed areas. More spots appeared and, even worse, he developed some cysts over his shoulders. Although he wasn't the worrying type he began to be alarmed by the size of the spots and his girlfriend brought matters to a head by saying that unless he did something about his acne she wasn't going to go out with him any more. It was clear to the doctor who saw David that the heat of the baking ovens was making his acne worse and he arranged for David to be temporarily transferred to a cooler job in the same company. This change and a prescription of a local retinoic acid preparation and oral treatment with tetracycline (see Chapter 5) brought a great improvement after two or three months. David has now resumed his original job at the ovens and has no acne.

## Clothing
Mostly your clothes will have no effect, good or bad, on acne, but there are some that can be a nuisance.

**Collars** The most obvious, I suppose, is a tight collar if you have acne of the neck. If you have inflamed acne spots around the neck a tight, and in particular a starched, collar may be very uncomfortable. It will probably make the spots even more sore, and the rubbing may even produce new

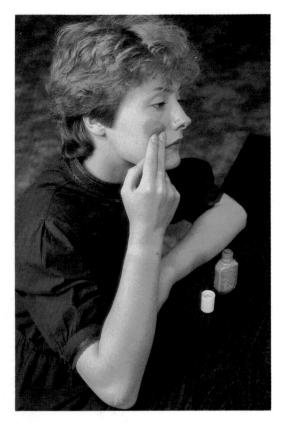

It isn't a good idea to wear thick, greasy make-up to disguise your spots.

spots. Woollen or fluffy collars also tend to irritate the skin and make existing acne worse.

**Jeans** Close-fitting, coarse denims may irritate your skin and cause acne spots in some rather unusual places (the buttocks and thighs, for example).

**Overalls** Grease and oil-soaked overalls are likely to cause an 'oil acne' on the thighs, the forearms, or wherever your skin is in contact with the oily clothing.

**Clothing that is very heavy** and makes you sweat a great deal is not the best type to wear if you have acne. In general the best clothing for you is the lightest and least fluffy that suits your lifestyle.

**Hats and helmets** Since acne spots develop frequently around the hairline, where greasy hair presses down on the skin (see Chapter 1), wearing tight or restrictive headgear such as motorbike helmets or uniform helmets will obviously make your acne worse.

# Conditions that may make your acne worse

The following conditions will not necessarily make your acne worse, but may affect a lot of you for part of the time.

### Monthly periods and the Pill

Many girls and young women develop spots just before and during their periods. In fact, the appearance of spots is like a signal for the start of their periods a few days later. The reason for this is as yet unknown, although it is probably due to a hormonal change which affects the skin.

The contraceptive pill has an unpredictable effect on acne because it's so much linked to the delicate hormone balance. Some girls' acne improves while they are taking it: in fact at one time the Pill was used as a form of treatment. But as they are made up of varying combinations of hormones not all contraceptive pills have the same effect. Besides not all girls with acne respond in the same way – some actually become worse while taking them – and so they are not now usually prescribed as a treatment. Hormone-like drugs (see page 68) are preferred today. In any case, the Pill is not usually recommended for women over thirty-five because there are possibly dangerous side effects for that age group. Although this is not the commonest group with acne, it is not unusual for women of this age to get spots around the time of their periods.

Janet was quite surprised to find that although she had had no acne as a teenager, at the age of thirty-five she was developing painful spots on her chin ten days or so before her periods. The spots subsided just before or at the time of the period. Nothing she bought from the chemist helped her blemishes and they resisted all the treatments that her doctor tried.

Although Janet's chin acne was not really very bad, she was extremely conscious of her spots as she believed that her success in her personnel management job depended on her immaculate appearance. She said that she had tried all sorts of vitamin pills and even ill-advisedly had a course of sunbed treatment, but the spots stubbornly returned each month.

Treatment with erythromycin tablets (see page 65) given by a colleague of mine did help a little but didn't suppress the condition completely. He told me that eventually he gave her treatment with a hormone preparation and this was successful.

## Cosmetics

Foundation creams and moisturizers may make your acne worse if you plaster your skin with the heaviest, greasiest preparation. If you use a foundation to mask your spots, it is probably better if it is of the medicated type (see page 36) so as not to aggravate the acne condition.

Acne can flare up at the most inconvenient times and you may not realize what is aggravating it. Melanie thought she was treating her skin well, while she was using cosmetics that made it a lot worse.

Acting was Melanie's chosen career. She had always had leading roles in school plays and had joined the local drama club when she left school. Although she hadn't succeeded in getting into a drama school she hoped to be 'noticed' eventually, and had been given a small part in the nearby professional pantomime the previous winter.

Melanie took what she believed to be tremendous care of her skin. She never used soap on her face as she had been told by her mother that it would destroy her complexion. She would remove the heavy, greasy stage make-up with a cream. She began to be troubled by many small acne spots over her face and used more thick stage make-up to hide them. Not unnaturally this made the spots worse.

Luckily an older woman in the cast recognized the problem before it got too out of hand. She knew that some people develop spots with stage make-up, just as Melanie had done, and explained to her that she must wash off all the make-up thoroughly. Melanie was reluctant to take the advice but in desperation washed her face with soap and water after removing the make-up with a cream, and she found that her complexion improved tremendously.

## Ointments

Just as you can get acne if you are in contact with oils and grease at work, so you can get it from using a skin ointment – perhaps for an infection or a cut – containing heavy oil or grease. Usually this doesn't happen if you wash the ointment off regularly. But if it is kept in close contact with your skin – especially with air-tight dressings – it can cause unpleasant acne where it is applied.

## Stress
I am frequently asked whether 'nerves' cause acne. By nerves my questioner usually means anxiety and/or stress. My answer is always that stress makes all sorts of medical conditions worse, including road traffic accidents and coronary heart disease. Of course acne is worsened by stress. It may even be brought on by stress, but it is not caused originally by stress. It is quite common for students to say that their acne worsens before and during examinations. You should note that eczema, psoriasis, indigestion and bowel disorders also become worse at such times. We don't really know all the connections between stress and disease but it seems that the body's defences are just not as good at this time as when you are in a rested and contented state.

# The myths

### Diet
Despite the old wives' tales, there is no evidence that chocolate causes acne! In fact some American researchers were so confident of this that to convince others they actually fed large amounts of chocolate to volunteers. The chocolate eaters may have felt sick but their acne didn't flare up. No one food can be blamed for the development or aggravation of acne and it would be interesting to know how the idea of food being a cause gained ground fifty or so years ago. It may have been part of the general idea that all illness is divine retribution and that munching naughty but enjoyable sweet or fatty foods resulted in this suitable punishment.

If you think about the way acne spots are caused (see Chapter 1) you will see that what you eat can't affect the number of spots you get. The rate at which your skin produces sebum, forming blackheads and spots, is not affected by fats, whether in chocolate or fried or other fatty foods. Sebum is made by your skin itself, and is not the same as the fats you eat. Neither can an excess of fat in your body 'ooze' into the hair follicles where the acne process is taking place.

### Life-style
Discos, lack of fresh air and irregular hours of sleep are sometimes blamed for ill health and the appearance of acne spots. It may seem a just punishment to an anxious and rather straitlaced parent that a wayward teenage son or daughter develops acne, but there is no evidence that living it up has any effect on the appearance or the course of acne – unless of course the activities of the teenager are so excessive that a complete physical

breakdown is likely. Acne should be no bar to living a completely normal life. Added restrictions and constraints are only likely to change a nuisance into a tragedy.

## Sex
Acne is not caused or made worse by any type of sexual activity. In Victorian times when any type of sexuality was publicly frowned upon, normal sexual urges became the cause of guilt feelings and considerable unhappiness. Masturbation was thought to be the cause of all sorts of things, including backache, cancer and acne! Of course there is absolutely no truth at all in these ideas.

# 3 CLEARING YOUR ACNE: WHAT YOU CAN DO

You have probably started using preparations to try and clear up your spots, and are taking some steps against getting more. In this chapter I explain which are the best, most effective ways to look after your skin and use treatments available over the counter and which are the methods and applications to avoid.

## Everyday treatment

### Keeping your skin clean – how important is it?

As you saw from Melanie's story in the last chapter, washing your face with soap is not harmful – in fact, to get rid of blackheads it is sensible to wash with soap and water sometimes, even if you usually use cleansers. However, washing more than usual is not necessary and will not actually improve acne or seborrhoea: you can't wash off acne spots, although to hear the advice of some grandmothers you wouldn't believe this! Washing with an antibacterial detergent-type solution may help mild acne by reducing the bacteria on the skin. But there is no, I repeat, NO evidence that washing either prevents acne or helps more severe types.

Most of the advice about washing seems to stem from the deep-rooted feeling that acne is due to 'dirt' (another myth! See page 14). Wiping the sebum off your skin may stop it looking shiny for a half hour or so but you cannot stop the oil glands from forming more. Continual washing and wiping will make the skin even more sore than it already is from the acne.

**Soap** If your skin is sensitive or sore because of acne or it is tender and inflamed, it is probably best to use a mild soap – for example, Simple Soap, Neutrogena or Oilatum soap. These are helpful because they will irritate your tender skin the least. Rinse your skin thoroughly and pat rather than rub it dry.

**Cleansing creams** If you are determined not to use soap on your face you should use only the lightest of cleansing milks and make sure you wipe off every trace afterwards.

**Astringent lotions** About ten years ago there was a great vogue for lotions that dissolved the surface grease on the skin and generally helped to clean

35

it, and they are still quite popular. They feel cool and leave the skin feeling fresher. They often contain the solvent acetone and also the astringent rose water. Although there is no evidence that removing the fatty sebum from the skin surface does any good in acne, it certainly doesn't do any harm. Common sense suggests that regular washing with soap will have the same result as the astringents; but it won't leave the same nice fresh feeling.

## Cosmetics

Many girls with acne are uncertain what to do about their cosmetics. Unfortunately it is not possible to be definite and say that you mustn't have this or that particular cosmetic, because people react in different ways to different cosmetics. However, a few guidelines should be useful.

**Foundations** I do not recommend you use heavy foundations as they seem to make acne worse and may even bring it on where you didn't have it before (see Chapter 2). But it is a good idea to try one of the non-greasy camouflage types if you want to cover up your spots. Otherwise, the camouflage sticks for applying to individual spots do not usually aggravate them – in fact they may actually have a soothing action. And some acne treatments are coloured so as to provide a kind of cosmetic effect (for example, Eskamel). I think these are good if the shade is right for you.

**Night creams, moisturizing creams and similar preparations** Certain mineral oils and waxes in these preparations can be troublesome. If you want to use one, you will just have to try out the different brands and see how they affect your acne. As a general rule, though, because your skin is likely to be oily already, you will probably do just as well without this type of skin preparation, or if you do use one, you will need only the lightest oil in water emulsion.

**Non-oily cosmetics** such as eye and lip make-up: these will not affect acne. Similarly, powders and rouge, perfumes and toilet waters cannot do any harm.

**Sun oils** A particular sort of acne with many small papules has been described as developing in Scandinavians using sun oils on holiday in Majorca. It isn't very common; but I don't recommend oily preparations as protection against the sun, rather a highly protective cream (see page 43) or non-greasy lotion.

## Hair preparations

Avoid using heavy hair greases, oils or conditioners. They make your hair oily and will probably produce spots on your forehead. If you already have fringe (bang) acne, they can make it worse. As with moisturizers, you are unlikely to need these preparations as your hair will already be greasy.

## Dandruff

Since your hair tends to be greasy if you have acne, owing to increased sebum secretion, you may also suffer from dandruff. This is because dandruff is believed to be caused by a little yeast-like bug that feeds on sebum, and it will of course flourish in greasy hair. There are special dandruff preparations available (for example, Head and Shoulders, Selsun and Lenium) that are effective in controlling the condition, as long as you follow the instructions carefully; and for your own comfort it is worth washing your hair regularly to keep the greasiness down. Any mild shampoo will do the job adequately.

Some people confuse other scalp conditions with dandruff. A few small white flakes on your shoulders may be just due to dryness or, if there is a lot of flaking, you may have psoriasis, another skin condition which needs treatment. Ask your doctor if in doubt.

## Shaving

The areas you shave, especially the chin, are also the places where your acne may be worst, and your skin particularly sensitive. When you have a very bad attack of spots you must obviously avoid shaving the affected areas until they calm down. Some young black men find close shaving very awkward as the hairs tend to bend back into the skin and cause even more irritation. If you have this trouble, it is best to grow a beard or just clip the hair. It doesn't matter whether you use wet shaving or an electric razor – though it may be a little kinder to your spots to use an electric razor if your face is very inflamed with acne.

Do not confuse these acne conditions with a shaving rash, which is an infection and needs treatment (see page 86).

## Clothes

I have already said that light, loose clothes are the most suitable for people with acne (see Chapter 2). You have probably discovered this yourself, but it's worth saying here that it is best to keep the affected parts of your body free from irritating fabrics such as coarse wool or harsh synthetic materials. Even in winter you can keep warm by wearing several loose layers of light clothing rather than tight or irritating garments. Try to avoid tight collars if you are liable to get acne spots on your neck as a rubbing collar can make the condition much worse.

## Environment

**Work** A hot, steamy or oily atmosphere undoubtedly does make acne worse so you should if possible avoid working in such conditions while your acne is bad (see Chapter 2).

**Cooking** Spending a long time in a hot, steamy kitchen can also be harmful, so if you are used to doing a lot of cooking, try to keep the window open to let as much steam as possible escape, and do not stand for hours over a deep fryer letting your face contact greasy fumes! While your acne is bad prepare meals that do not require long and intricate stages of cooking.

**Recreation** The same advice applies to places you go to enjoy yourself. Discos, pubs, and hot, crowded cinemas will not exactly help your skin condition. But you certainly shouldn't give up your social life for the sake of acne spots. Just remember to dress lightly while inside and give yourself a few minutes in the fresh air from time to time if you start getting uncomfortably sweaty.

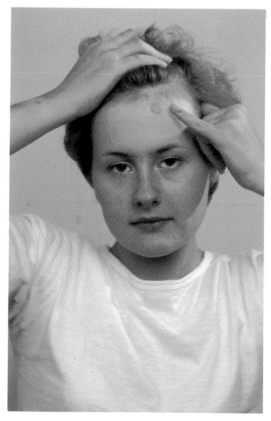

There are some excellent medicated foundations that will mask your spots effectively.

Avoid cooking in a greasy, steamy atmosphere if you have acne.

# Does sunlight help acne?

Many young people tell me that their acne improves in the summertime after they have exposed their skin to the sun. Unfortunately the improvement is only short-lived, during holidays. It is no answer to try and extend the effect by blasting your skin continually with large amounts of possibly harmful artificial sunlight. The sun and artificial sunlight can do considerable damage in the long term.

### How does sunlight work in acne?

What is it about sunlight that helps to suppress acne? The answer is that it is only a very small portion of the sun's rays that have this action – the part of sunlight known as ultraviolet light. Ultraviolet light is the part of the sun's spectrum just beyond the blue-violet portion and is itself divided into three parts. The part nearest to violet light is known as long-wave ultraviolet light (known as ultraviolet light A or just UVA). The short-wave ultraviolet light (UVB) and the very short-wave ultraviolet (UVC) follow in turn. Sunburn and tanning is caused mainly by UVB, though UVA may play some part – particularly in tanning. The very short wave

A hot, smoky disco will be uncomfortable so give yourself a breather from time to time.

does not seem to be important because most of it is absorbed out of the sun's rays in the atmosphere above the earth.

Sunlamps can be made to supply UVA or UVB, but most lamps give out mainly UVB, and it is the UVB that seems helpful in acne.

How does the ultraviolet light work in acne? It certainly produces a peel, like the peeling and abrasive agents I describe later (see page 47) which gets rid of the horny skin and blackheads that are such an important feature of acne. But it is thought that ultraviolet light has other properties too which help in acne. These may affect the bacteria of the skin and even the rate of sebum secretion.

## What are the dangers of sunlight?
Even if ultraviolet light helps acne, it can have some unpleasant effects over long periods. Most of the changes in the skin that we think are due to ageing are in fact the result of damage to the skin from the sun's ultraviolet rays. If you are fair-skinned or are exposed to the sun for long periods, your skin will begin to look older much earlier than if you have a dark complexion, are not much of a sun lover and do not work out of doors. I know that most girls don't want to end up by looking like wrinkled

prunes – and this can happen if they have too much sun.

Even worse news is to come! Too much sunlight on your skin over long periods can lead to small growths. Mostly the growths that occur are not very serious, but they can be disfiguring and certainly can damage the health.

It is not my aim to alarm you or send you rushing out to buy broad-brimmed hats or sunscreens in the middle of winter, but I do think that there is not enough thought given to the possible dangers of too much sun. Obviously we are all keen on the sun, and a little is good for everyone. But the sun worshippers should take heed. Don't forget that golden tan will eventually give way to ugly wrinkling.

**Protecting your skin**
If you are planning a holiday in the sun you may be keen to take advantage of the sunlight to improve your acne. But please do be careful to avoid getting burnt. Here are a few tips:

- Avoid greasy sun oils – although they may protect against sunburn they are sometimes to blame for an outbreak of acne spots (see page 36).

Ultraviolet light in moderate doses can clear spots, but follow the experts' advice.

Sunlight may help but beware of getting sunburnt, even when lying in partial shade.

- Buy a sunscreen lotion with a high sun protection factor (SPF). A sun protection factor of 12 or more will allow most people out in the bright sun for at least a few minutes without being burnt.

- Remember that a sun protecting cream that guards against very hot sun for long periods has not been invented yet. Whether you have put on a sunscreen or not, spend only a few minutes in the sun at first and then gradually increase the time that you are exposed, day by day.

- Don't forget that you can be burnt quite easily through thin blouses or shirts, and that what seems to be a shady place may actually be exposed to quite a lot of ultraviolet light from reflection. The sea, the sand and light-coloured buildings all reflect the sun's rays extremely well, so that if you are sitting on the beach under a palm tree you are not only in danger of being walloped on the head by a coconut but also of receiving a nasty sunburn!

Some people with acne are too embarrassed to take off their shirts or

Ultraviolet light, beyond the spectrum, is divided into three sections.

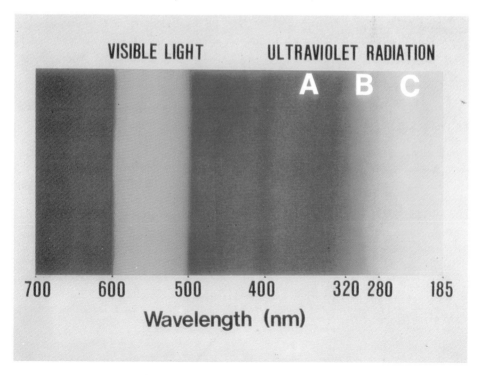

blouses to sunbathe because of the spots on their shoulders, chest or back. If you feel that way, remember acne is a common condition and everyone has had acne spots at some time. There is no point in being shy about it; it will only spoil your enjoyment.

### The dangers of sunlamps

I do not advise you to rush out and buy the first sunlamp that you see. Ultraviolet treatment doesn't suit everyone – we don't know why some acne sufferers are helped and some are not, but it is well known that we all differ in the way we react to sunlight. Fair-skinned people with blue eyes can be badly burnt by long exposure to ultraviolet light. If you buy a lamp yourself, start treatment very cautiously and according to the manufacturers' instructions. But I believe that it is unwise to use a sunlamp without proper advice from a doctor. Many hospitals have facilities for ultraviolet light treatment, and if your doctor feels that it will be right for you he or she will make the necessary arrangements. This is the best way of having the treatment if you need it. It is given by experts with the right type of equipment and you do not have the expense of buying the lamp or the danger of using it in an inexpert way.

### Sunbeds

One further word before I leave ultraviolet light. Various types of sunbeds have become popular for getting a tan. It has also been suggested that they may be a good treatment for acne. My own view is that they are unnecessary and possibly harmful in the long term as they add to the total dose of UV light received by the skin. Anyway, I think women are prettier pink than when they are an artificial sort of yellow-brown! Fortunately, the fashion writers seem to be thinking along those lines now too.

# Diet

As I said on page 33 there is nothing to be gained from changing your diet. Of course it is unhealthy to eat a large amount of sweets and chocolates or to stuff yourself with fried foods, cakes, pastries and biscuits. Common sense will tell you that a balanced diet containing lean meat, fish, fresh vegetables, fibre and fruit as well as moderate quantities of dairy produce can only be helpful to your health generally, although it may not make much difference to your acne.

# Blackheads and spots – should you squeeze them?

There is a great temptation to pick and pull at your skin when you have spots. Some doctors rationalize this tendency by actually encouraging

44

people with acne to search for blackheads and remove them by using a blackhead extractor (these can be bought in most pharmacies or drug stores), and to prick the tops of the pus spots with a clean needle. I do not think this does much to get rid of the acne and if anything, I discourage people from fiddling with their skin in this way. Although scars from acne spots eventually disappear, fiddling, squeezing and scratching pustules is going to mark your skin to begin with, and there is nothing to be gained from trying to get rid of your spots this way.

If you can't resist fiddling, at least restrict yourself to getting the blackheads out, as this will leave no scars, and before you start make sure your hands and nails are scrupulously clean. Gently steaming your face before you start may help as it softens the horny layer of the skin and so makes the blackheads easier to remove.

Now that I have talked about the practical measures you can take to help get rid of your acne, I shall describe what medical treatments you can buy without a prescription anywhere that cosmetics and toiletries are sold, and which I think are effective (a few may only be available at pharmacies or drug stores).

Using an extractor is a better way of getting rid of blackheads than picking.

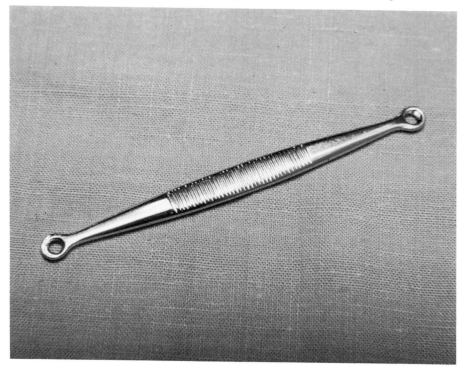

# Treatments available over the counter

If you have mild acne and you don't want to bother your doctor, you may well decide that you will get something from the pharmacist. Or you may see an advertisement suggesting that you can rid yourself of your spots by using a particular cream or lotion and decide to give it a try. If you follow this course you should bear a few points in mind.

### Choose the right preparation
There are four groups of preparations you can choose from:

1. Those containing drugs which are also present in the creams or lotions your doctor might prescribe (benzoyl peroxide, resorcinol or sulphur; I describe the action of these drugs in Chapter 5).

2. Those that rely on antiseptics to kill bacteria on your skin.

3. Abrasive agents which rid your skin of blackheads.

4. Other preparations working in different ways (for example, ethyl lactate treatment).

### Preparations containing special drugs
These are stronger than the other three groups and will be a better choice during a particularly bad outbreak of spots. Try to find out what the preparation you decide to buy contains. If it has none of the substances listed above, you may be wasting your money. When in doubt ask the pharmacist, who will usually know a great deal about most of the treatments he or she sells.

You must remember that these substances may have side effects, especially irritation of your skin. This applies particularly to creams and lotions containing benzoyl peroxide or sulphur (see Chapter 5). Both of these can help – but they can make your skin feel sore at the same time. Remember that your face skin is more sensitive than the skin on the chest and back. Your chest may be able to withstand 10 per cent benzoyl peroxide but your facial skin may only be able to have 5 per cent applied without burning.

### Antiseptics and other bacterial agents
There are huge numbers of antiseptic soaps, creams and lotions available for treating acne. They contain one or another substance that kills bacteria on the skin surface and in the hair follicles (see page 16). The antiseptics (it's more accurate to call them non-antibiotic antibacterial agents, or just antibacterial agents) include such substances as hexachlorophane, povidone-iodine (Betadine) and hydroxyquinoline. They do have a helpful effect on

acne but it doesn't seem to be very great, so they are suitable for treating mild outbreaks of acne only. They take up to three or four weeks, or longer, to make any improvement, so do persist once you've started using one of these treatments.

Antibacterial agents can irritate the skin but are much less likely to do so than the drug treatments I mention above containing benzoyl peroxide or sulphur. Antibacterial agents can also cause an allergic sensitivity reaction – but this is really quite uncommon.

### Abrasive agents

As blocked hair follicles seem so important in starting acne, then unblocking them should help. This is at least part of the purpose of some of the anti-acne creams and lotions described above. There are also preparations that try to get rid of blackheads and so unblock follicles more directly. They literally try to sandpaper off the tops of the blackheads and so loosen them.

Lotions (for example, Ionax Scrub), or pastes (Brasivol) that contain

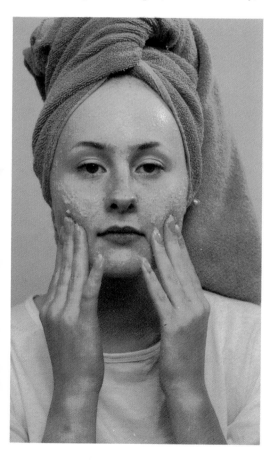

An abrasive lotion can be very effective in clearing blackheads.

very small but hard particles are used instead of sandpaper! You can confirm their similarity to sandpaper yourself by rubbing the materials between your fingers to feel their grittiness. Apart from these preparations, abrasive sponges are also available which do the same job (for example, Bufpufs).

Stronger agents known as keratolytics that loosen blackheads in a different way are contained in some lotions that can be bought over the counter (for example, Acnil, Clearasil Cream Medication, Medac Acne Cream, Dermaclear). I describe these in more detail in Chapter 5 as they are important in treatments your doctor may prescribe.

Abrasive agents have the advantage of being very safe treatments, although if used too vigorously they can make the skin slightly sore. If you have a great accumulation of blackheads, these treatments may help. But they are not likely to be the right treatment for anyone with inflamed acne.

### Different treatments

It would be impossible to talk about all the substances used in every acne treatment. But it is worthwhile describing some not already mentioned. Astringent and detergent lotions are popular – they make you feel less greasy although they have no lasting effect on acne. You can buy mild drugs to damp down inflammation but I don't think these treatments you can buy yourself are very helpful.

Recently a new approach using the compound lactate has been developed. The idea is to increase the acids inside the hair follicles and in that way prevent the chemical reactions that take place there. This is intended to stop the irritating products of these reactions being made so that the inflammation decreases. The lotion that has been developed contains 10 per cent of ethyl lactate and 0.3 per cent of zinc sulphate in an alcohol-type lotion (its commercial name is Triac). The makers claim that it is as effective as 5 per cent benzoyl peroxide preparations but does not cause the irritation that they often do (see Chapter 5). They also say that inflammation decreases quickly, and the redness around the acne spots disappeared in half the people they have tested within twenty-four hours! Improvements in the long term also seem satisfactory.

This treatment is on direct sale to the public in the UK but cannot be prescribed at present.

### Don't waste your money

There seems to be a little voice in many of us that whispers that the more you pay for a product the better it is likely to be. Nothing could be further from the truth. There are some very good cheap preparations, and if these do the trick there is no reason to spend more. Some of the expensive products are beautifully presented and delicately perfumed but in general they don't have many other advantages.

## How long should you continue treatment?

No cream or lotion works immediately. Indeed it may be several weeks before some applications seem even to start working. It makes no sense to chop and change preparations without giving any of them a fair chance.

If your acne does not improve after two months then it is time to make an appointment with your doctor. If it not only fails to improve but seems to become rapidly worse you should try to see the doctor as soon as possible.

## 'Natural' remedies

As I said on page 46, you should be cautious about buying remedies for acne that do not list any special ingredient recommended by the medical profession as effective. Be particularly wary of herbal remedies and 'natural remedy' products. They usually cost a great deal and I have no evidence that they improve acne spots to any significant degree. Much the same applies to treatments by non-medically qualified practitioners.

There is no reason why, if you have mild acne and don't want to go to your doctor about it, you should not be able to clear it up by following the advice in this chapter. All you need is the basic knowledge and your own common sense. In Chapter 5 I describe the stronger treatments your doctor will prescribe if your acne is more severe, or you just haven't been successful yourself. But first I want to talk about the effect having acne has on your relationships – with the opposite sex, with your friends and family.

# 4 YOU AND OTHER PEOPLE

Acne is not a disorder like measles that comes and goes within a month. It lasts for months and even years. To those that have it, it seems to last for ever! Not only do the spots apparently come and go for ages but the effects of the spots – the scars – last even longer. Under these circumstances you have to come to terms with your acne. You have to develop ways of coping with everyday life. In this chapter I will try to give some simple hints on how to deal with some problems that may arise in living with acne.

## Other people's attitudes to acne

Acne mainly affects people between the ages of thirteen and twenty-five – just the time of life when you are beginning to stand on your own feet and learning to make lasting relationships. Sensibility to insult and to being spurned is highest during these years. And yet people do not tend to be sympathetic. 'Spotty', 'Poxy', 'Scabby' are some of the least unpleasant names shouted after unfortunate people with any blemish on their skin. Of course this causes a lot of unhappiness and tension in the person affected.

It is a curious fact that there is a deep fear of skin disease in everyone. It is important that you realize this so that you can at least understand why those boorish people around you are jeering at your discomfort. Presumably the primitive reaction dates back to the time when hygiene did not exist and there were no treatments for skin disorders – it must have been a defensive act by the community to cast out the affected person. You have probably heard about the leprosy sufferers in the Middle Ages who had to ring a bell as they entered a normal community so that healthy people would not risk infection by coming near them. Today we call this attitude to skin disease the leper complex. I want to emphasize that this primitive fear is in us all, even medical students and student nurses. I always try to teach them in training that there is no reason for the disgust they feel. Most of the rashes and spots which skin specialists deal with are not infectious or contagious – and certainly acne is not.

Of course, to understand people's reactions to your acne spots is not to enjoy it, but it does help a bit. You should remember that your acne is at least proof that you have sex hormones in your blood! In fact, one of my colleagues has gone so far as to suggest that acne is not really a disease at all but a sign of sexual readiness – he calls it a 'sexual traffic light'.

## The opposite sex

Obviously for most of you your attractiveness to the opposite sex is of prime importance and you will be striving for perfection as far as your 'body image' is concerned. You want a slim, perfectly proportioned body and a blemish-free skin – to be like the stars on film and television. Yet at this very time your acne is likely to be at its worst.

When you feel your acne is your worst problem, remember that everyone of your age is striving after the same, completely unattainable ideal. Everybody has imperfections, some more noticeable than others. It is just the way that human beings are constructed: we are not the same on both sides – the right-hand side of the face differs from the left-hand side. We all have moles and other sorts of birthmarks. Some people have more hair than others. But everyone is attracted by different looks. 'There is someone for everyone', I have heard it said, and I am sure that this is pretty well

Don't stay at home by yourself – that's likely to make you feel more depressed about your acne.

the truth. So there is just no point in becoming obsessed about one or other feature on your face. Your spots are not as unattractive as you think!

You may dread going to parties or discos because you'll be meeting new people of the opposite sex and worry that they won't like you. Don't be put off by that – remember, you're unlikely to be the only one with spots. You'll find that having acne does not in the end stop someone of the opposite sex making a pass. Interestingly enough, several well-known television and film stars are quite obviously scarred with acne!

## Your friends

What I have said about the opposite sex applies equally to friends and acquaintances of your own sex and age. Remember, they are just as concerned to make a good impression as you are, and probably have other worries about their appearance. If they make jibes at you, don't take it as an excuse to be nasty in return; although it might be tempting it doesn't make for great friendships, and it doesn't get any of you any further! It is much more lastingly satisfying to ignore the taunts as if they didn't bother you at all. You'll find then that they eventually fade away, as your acne itself will in time.

## Your family

Your parents will probably react sympathetically to your feelings about having acne so long as you don't make it a major tragedy at home. Don't expect everlasting patience: after all, they have their own worries and strains so they can't be expected to put up with constant moaning. Once you've voiced your unhappiness, you'll probably find you get more help and sympathy if you don't keep on mentioning your problem; the same applies in the case of brothers and sisters. However, if you ever feel you are becoming obsessed by your condition and really feel very anxious or depressed, you must of course seek help and you will probably go to your parents and discuss it with them first, before consulting the doctor.

Of course, you may be unlucky and find your parents are not as sympathetic as you would hope. Don't be too critical of them – remember their criticism of your spots may be due to their old-fashioned views about the cause. In Susan's case, her parents needed the doctor's advice as well as she did.

Susan first developed a few spots when she was fourteen but these did not trouble her very much at first. Her spots got worse when she was working hard for school-leaving exams. She bought a cream from a pharmacy and this seemed to help for a few weeks, but then the spots

52

gradually increased in number and size. Susan became very sensitive to remarks about her skin, especially when they came from her parents. Her father in particular used to annoy her by suggesting that if she spent more time at school work and less with her friends at parties her skin would improve! Her mother didn't help by saying that she should take more trouble about washing her face.

Susan was eventually taken to the doctor, who saw that most of the problem was in the relationship between Susan and her parents. He tried to straighten things out by explaining that Susan's acne was not as bad as they all thought and that it was certainly not due to any wickedness or lack of hygiene. He gave Susan tetracycline tablets and a benzoyl peroxide containing gel. Unfortunately she used the treatment irregularly and then gave it up after three or four weeks. Not unexpectedly she didn't improve greatly and became upset and depressed about her spotty complexion and began picking and squeezing her pimples.

After some weeks Susan's doctor referred her to a hospital dermatology clinic. The importance of regular and persistent treatment was explained and I am pleased to say that Susan's acne cleared up and she was able to have a spot-free eighteenth birthday party.

# Your job

If you have a job which means you have to meet the public or deal with customers, having acne on the face can be quite embarrassing for you. You should remember that you are far more conscious of your spots than the customers are. If you are very worried by the spots you can disguise them with special cosmetics (see Chapter 3). On no account should you start changing your job to one that seems more protected – even if you could – as this would not provide a solution but rather increase your feeling of being an outcast.

Of course you should take steps to treat your acne and with this and a little understanding you will probably find your worries fade. However, once again I do advise that if you really cannot stop worrying you ought to talk your problem over with your doctor.

# Beware of advice

Well-meaning relatives and friends are often full of advice and suggestions. My guess is that if you have acne yourself you will have discovered this already. I believe that this is one of the most difficult and trying aspects of having a really common disorder. Few of us welcome this type of help. A whole book could be written about the various folk remedies for acne and how the ideas for the particular treatments arose. Usually (but not always!) the advice is well-meaning and may be based on a particular treatment known to have helped somebody else.

Grandmothers seem to be particularly strong on advice but unfortunately their wisdom doesn't always match their years. Listen politely to any suggestions and then think about them carefully. Just because rhubarb seemed to help Jenny's bad teenage spots it doesn't follow that it will help yours.

Several points have to be remembered. First, not everyone reacts in the same way to the same treatment. No one knows why some people are helped by one and why others are helped by another. In fact, what seems to help one person can make another worse. Second, the belief of the person giving advice, that a particular treatment was successful for someone they knew, may be quite wrong. It may have been pure chance that Jenny's acne improved when she took rhubarb. Research scientists know that you cannot rely on one observation – that is why trials with many people are required to discover whether one remedy is better than another.

Advice in advertisements also has to be accepted cautiously. Remember it is given for one very good reason – to make you buy the particular treatment advertised. This does not mean that what an advertisement says

Discuss your worries with your doctor if you really can't get over feeling depressed.

is completely untrue. But it does mean that those who advertise are likely to present their products in the best possible light, without mentioning either disadvantages or that not everyone will be helped.

Another point to bear in mind before taking someone's advice about acne treatments is one I have mentioned elsewhere: no remedy works immediately. Give any treatment you are currently using a fair chance before changing to something else. Some treatments (for example, tetracycline – see Chapter 5) take up to four or five months before having their best effect.

It is always wise to listen to the advice that well-meaning friends, colleagues, relatives and advertisements give, but rarely is it wise to follow that advice without a great deal of thought. When in doubt take the problem to your doctor; his advice will be based on knowledge and considerable experience.

# Dealing with depression

All I have said about how people react to your acne can affect your state of mind to a greater or lesser degree. Some particularly sensitive people tend to get quite disturbed by their acne. When groups of acne sufferers have been investigated for their psychological 'profile' it has been found that they often are quite depressed in the clinical sense. Well, this is hardly surprising. Acne is an unpleasant disorder that persists and can be quite sore and painful. Luckily, most of you snap out of being depressed about your acne fairly quickly when you realize it won't last for ever. But if your depression hangs around and you just can't enjoy yourself in any way and can't forget your problem, you should seek assistance from your doctor. There is just no point in storing up all your unhappiness in yourself. Discussion with someone sensible whom you can trust, such as your doctor, can only be helpful.

# 5 GOING TO THE DOCTOR

It is of course up to you if or when you decide to see a doctor but there are some circumstances that I believe particularly need the advice and treatment of a doctor: if your acne has progressively worsened over a few weeks or months is one; the appearance of large painful spots can make life miserable and requires medical treatment. And I strongly recommend that you seek medical advice if you think your acne has reached a stage at which you cannot control it and which may lead to scarring. You also need to see your doctor if the condition of your skin is interfering with your work or your social life. Medical advice can be very helpful too if acne is making you anxious or depressed.

## Treatments for acne

There are many different treatments for acne that your doctor can recommend. They include drug treatments, physical treatments and surgical treatments. I will deal with the ones that you are most likely to have prescribed.

## Drug treatments

In this section I will attempt to outline the main drug treatments available and say a little about the way they work. In general they fall into the following groups:

- Those that are designed to cut down the bacteria in the follicles and on the skin

- Those meant to unblock hair follicles by getting rid of blackheads

- Those that cut down the rate of sebum secretion

- Treatments that are thought to cut down the inflammation associated with acne

- Drugs which combine more than one of these actions.

My guess is that most of the readers of this book will think of treatments for acne in a different way. They will think of two sorts of treatment – those that are put on the acne spots themselves and those that are taken by mouth, and this is the way I'll divide them and describe them.

# Treatments that are put on the spots – local treatments

These are sometimes known as local or topical treatments. Whether they are effective depends so much on your skin condition, your type of acne and other factors in your body make-up that it is difficult for a doctor to know immediately which one is best for you. So you may have to try several treatments before there is a noticeable improvement in your skin. That will not be because your doctor doesn't know what he is doing, but because different people's reactions to the various treatments is unpredictable. If you get a dry, irritated skin, for example, the prescription may have to be changed.

Local treatments are made of an active chemical compound (drug) and the 'vehicle' substance in which the drug is dissolved or suspended. Local treatments for acne are usually lotions, creams or gels. Gels are transparent, glassy, jelly-like materials that seem to disappear when they are put on the skin because they are made mostly of water. Ointments are only very occasionally used as greasy applications can make acne worse. Pastes are used slightly more frequently than ointments. They are thick and not very greasy.

You should always put local treatments for acne over all the affected areas once or twice a day, according to directions – it's no use expecting treatment applied to the forehead to help the spots on your back!

### Treatments containing benzoyl peroxide

In recent years benzoyl peroxide preparations have become very popular in the treatment of acne. In fact, benzoyl peroxide is the mainstay of modern local treatment and it's difficult to know how we managed before it came along about thirty years ago. One of its main actions is to kill bacteria. It does this by giving up some of the oxygen it contains, so benzoyl peroxide is especially effective in killing anaerobic bacteria (see Chapter 1). It also loosens blackheads so that follicles become unblocked, which is probably an important part of its healing effect.

Benzoyl peroxide is made up into creams, lotions and gels (for example, AcetOxy Gel, Acnegel, Debroxide, Benoxyl, Panoxyl, Theraderm). Most of the preparations contain it in a concentration of 5 per cent, although some are as strong as 10 per cent and others as weak as 2.5 per cent. The particular product prescribed for you by the doctor will depend on how your acne, and your skin, respond. There are some preparations which combine other antibacterial substances with benzoyl peroxide (for example, Quinoderm) in an attack on all fronts!

Usually one daily application of a preparation containing benzoyl peroxide is sufficient, but two daily applications may be recommended for people with stubborn acne. The treatment starts to improve the spots within two or three weeks and the improvement usually increases for the next few weeks.

Most people with acne find that their spots do improve with preparations containing benzoyl peroxide. If the condition is mild it may be the only treatment needed. Even when the condition is more than mild and there are deep papules, this treatment is often effective. The main reason for it failing is that people forget to put the preparation on regularly. It does seem important to apply it every day.

**Side effects** People using benzoyl peroxide often find that their skin becomes a little dry and rougher, but they can tolerate it quite well – especially as it is obviously doing them some good. But unfortuately in a few the dryness is more pronounced. Their skin becomes very dry, pink and scaling where they have applied the preparation. This drying effect may be so severe that the surface of the skin actually cracks. Blonds and redheads seem most at risk from severe irritation – they have a sensitive skin to all sorts of things, including the sun.

Apart from this irritation the drug really is very safe.

To counteract the irritating effect that benzoyl peroxide can have, some preparations contain hydrocortisone as well as the benzoyl peroxide (for example, Quinoderm-hydrocortisone – see page 62). The hydrocortisone is supposed to help by damping down the inflammation.

If your skin reacts strongly to the preparation your doctor has prescribed, you should tell him immediately and he will find something better suited to you.

### Sulphur treatments

Sulphur is a very old medical treatment. Like benzoyl peroxide, sulphur does kill bacteria and other micro-organisms and mites, and this is probably the way it clears up acne, although even now we are not certain exactly how it works. However, it does have other effects on the skin as well, as it also seems to help certain other types of skin condition, including eczema. It is possible that it works in other ways too, by loosening blackheads so that they are no longer blocking the follicles, and by causing the skin to peel.

Sulphur is used in concentrations of from 1 to 6 per cent in lotions, creams, gels and pastes. Including sulphur in a preparation gives it a slightly yellowish colour and a faint, sharp smell. Sometimes, when the smell is stronger, it seems like rotten eggs. In my experience acne treatments that contain sulphur can be of great help to people with fairly mild acne and I usually prescribe a sulphur preparation as an alternative for anyone whose skin reacts to benzoyl peroxide. The blackheads, small pus spots and tiny papules start to improve after about a week and improvement can continue for another two or three weeks.

Some dermatologists do not use sulphur treatments because they believe that more blackheads appear after their use. This has not so far happened to anyone for whom I've prescribed sulphur.

**Sulphur compounds** In some creams and lotions sulphur is combined with other substances in order to increase the overall effect. One preparation is very old-fashioned but can be quite effective. This is sulphur and resorcinol paste. Sulphated potash lotion (Kummerfeld's Lotion) is another 'old timer' which is still prescribed (and is successful, I am told). I don't give it to my patients because it smells so awful!

**Side effect** Some people cannot tolerate preparations containing sulphur, even in quite low concentrations, as their skin becomes scaly, pink and sore after using them. So you see, there are many similarities between sulphur and benzoyl peroxide in treating acne.

### Vitamin A type treatments
Some lotions and gels containing retinoids, that is, compounds derived from Vitamin A, are used in the treatment of acne. They work by loosening the blackheads and making them pop out.

The most effective local treatment currently available is retinoic acid. It is put in a 0.025 per cent concentration in a gel and 0.05 per cent concentration in a cream.

These preparations seem more popular in North America than in Europe or Australia. I don't know why this is so, but as with many other things, we are almost certain to follow the trend in a few years' time. It is also likely that other retinoids will be developed for local use in the not too distant future.

**Side effect** Retinoic acid makes some people's skin quite sore after it has been used for a few days. The treated areas become pink and slightly dry and scaly. This is a tremendous shame because the treatment is quite effective.

Olwen's story shows how local treatments may irritate a sensitive skin.

She had a typically Celtic skin with a light complexion, blue eyes and reddish hair. Her skin burnt easily in the sun and she said that her skin was always very sensitive. When she developed a few acne pimples on her forehead and chin she used an acne lotion she had bought from the toilet goods counter of the local supermarket, and was upset to find that it brought her out in a rash – worse than the original spots. That took her to her doctor, who prescribed first a benzoyl peroxide cream, then a sulphur lotion and finally a retinoic acid gel. Each one made her skin red, sore and scaly. Olwen became quite upset by all this and eventually dropped every form of treatment. The rashes cleared but her spots stubbornly remained. She was seen by a skin specialist who realized that she was one of those people with an extremely sensitive skin. He prescribed a mild cleansing lotion with an antiseptic in it and a very low concentration sulphur preparation. These treatments helped Olwen's acne and although they made her skin peel a little they did not make it as sore as the other treatments, and she was able to tolerate them.

## Antibiotic treatments in creams and lotions

The antibiotics that have been used in creams and lotions for acne include erythromycin, clindamycin, tetracycline, chlormycetin and neomycin. The last two of these have been in preparations available in the United Kingdom for some time. Preparations containing erythromycin, clindamycin and tetracycline are more recent and are currently still only available for prescription in North America. These newer preparations have been specially formulated so that they can penetrate the skin.

According to doctors who have had experience with these antibiotic preparations they are quite effective for the milder types of acne. The main advantages are that they don't irritate the skin, they are clean and don't show when they are put on. Like benzoyl peroxide and sulphur preparations, they work by attacking the bacteria on the skin.

**Side effects** I must admit that I am not yet convinced that local antibiotics have a great deal more to offer than other types of acne creams and lotions; and they do present some problems. Although they do not irritate the skin they can cause skin problems. Some people develop an allergy to the antibiotic and break out in an eczema. This is fairly uncommon, but the rash is likely to be worse than the soreness and irritation caused by benzoyl peroxide and sulphur preparations. It persists longer and spreads over a larger area of skin.

This sensitivity eczema is not the only problem. A big objection is that the wide use of local antibiotics may cause what is known as bacterial resistance in the bacteria on the skin. This doesn't matter too much for the person being treated but does matter for the general community. The danger is that the bacteria that have become resistant can spread to other people. What is worse is that the resistance to the one antibiotic used can cause resistance to certain other antibiotics; and not only that – it seems that the antibiotic resistance itself may spread to other (possibly more dangerous) bacteria. If this happens we could end up with more diseases caused by bacteria resistant to whole groups of antibiotics, which could be very difficult to treat. None of this has so far happened, but the possibility is a nightmare for researchers working on bacteria – and one that I sincerely hope never comes true.

Although the same argument can apply to the use of antibiotics given by mouth (see page 63), the risks appear fewer and this form of treatment seems more justifiable. First, when given by mouth there is slightly less risk of the resistant bacteria spreading. Second, antibiotics taken in tablet or capsule form are given for more severe forms of acne, for which there are few other treatments – in contrast to local antibiotics which are given for the milder forms, for which there are other treatments anyway.

## Keratolytic treatments that cause desquamation (peeling)

Drugs which encourage your blackheads to pop out of their follicles or to disintegrate and unblock the follicles are called comedolytic agents. Most of these materials make the surface horn on the skin desquamate (peel off) as well, and so are also known as keratolytic agents. Some keratolytics are less effective than others in getting rid of blackheads and we really don't know why. However, as they do have some effect they are occasionally included in preparations containing other substances to increase the whole effect.

One of these keratolytics is salicylic acid. This is very efficient in getting rid of scale or smoothing down an area of hard skin in other skin diseases. It comes in concentrations of 2 to 6 per cent, or even higher sometimes. It is usually put in concentrations of 2 per cent in preparations for acne. Close relatives of salicylic acid are the salicylates which you may recognize as drugs you use for headaches and other minor aches and pains (aspirin is acetyl salicylic acid). Although they belong to the same group of drugs their pain-relieving action does not seem to be related to the keratolytic action, neither do they have a keratolytic action.

Among other substances which seem to have a peeling action and are sometimes included in acne treatments is resorcin. This is combined with sulphur in the old-fashioned sulphur and resorcin paste (see page 59). It seemed to produce considerable soreness as well as a peel and I do not think there is much place for it now. Betanaphthol was another agent once used that produced peeling, but again there seems no particular advantage to prescribing it now that we have more effective and gentle treatments.

## Corticosteroids

These are hormone-type drugs like cortisone that are given for conditions such as rheumatoid arthritis in which there is continual inflammation. They can be given as tablets, local preparations or injections. As acne spots are inflamed (see Chapter 1), I am often asked whether it is right to use corticosteroid creams or ointments for acne. The answer is 'No'. These preparations do little good for acne and may do considerable harm. In fact, some of the stronger ones can actually cause acne and they can have other unpleasant side effects too.

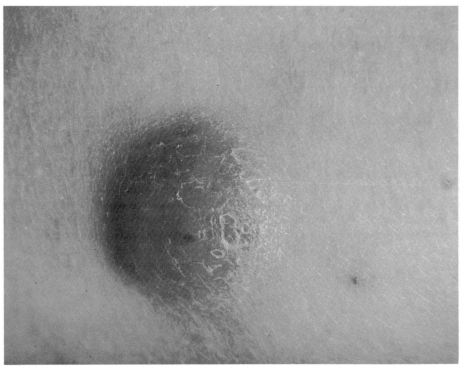
Large cysts of this type can be treated by injection.

However, there are exceptions to this general rule:

- Hydrocortisone is a mild type of corticosteroid preparation and when benzoyl peroxide is causing some soreness it may help to use a treatment containing both benzoyl peroxide and hydrocortisone (Quinoderm-hydrocortisone).

- Acne cysts and very prominent acne scars are occasionally improved by injecting small quantities of a steroid directly into the affected area (see page 71).

- The only other occasion when I think it is right to use these drugs for acne is in a very severe and inflamed case such as acne fulminans (see page 79).

# Oral treatments (treatments given by mouth)

Tablets, pills, capsules or medicines are given by doctors generally for the more severe forms of acne. In tablets the active drug is contained in some other powdery substance which is formed into the shape of the tablet. Pills are very similar but have a sugary coating on the outside. Capsules have a softish gelatine-type outer cover, inside which there is a powder containing the drug itself. Medicines are liquids that have the drug either dissolved or suspended in them.

### Oral versus local treatments: what are the advantages?

When a drug is given by mouth for acne it reaches other parts of your body as well as your skin and may have side effects. This is why some doctors are uneasy about prescribing powerful drugs by mouth for a skin condition.

Apart from this possible problem, oral drugs do have the great advantage in treating more severe acne of avoiding local treatment. Many people with acne don't much like putting creams, pastes or lotions on their skin: they are not keen on using them because they may show and then there is the difficulty of reaching the back – a favourite site for acne. Unless you can persuade a parent or friend to put the treatment on, you may find that it stays in the container!

### The antibiotics – how do they work?

There are large numbers of antibiotics but only a few of them are used in the treatment of acne. One theory as to how they work is that they cut down the growth of the bacteria on the skin and this obviously reduces the amount of fat splitting the bacteria can do (see page 16). But the length of time the antibiotics take to act and the relatively small dose needed have led some researchers to doubt whether this is the whole answer. There are several other theories. One of them is that the antibiotics reduce the amount of fat splitting itself, rather than the growth of the bacteria. Another suggestion is that the antibiotics calm down the inflammation in the spots by stopping some of the white blood cells from reaching the inflamed areas.

As you see, there is no clear-cut answer to the question 'How do antibiotics work in acne?' I think that this is a very important area for further research as if we are sure about how a treatment works it is possible to develop other and more efficient drugs.

### The tetracyclines

The antibiotics that are most often prescribed are a group called the tetracyclines. They are available in tablets, pills, capsules and medicines. The main ones used for acne are tetracycline, oxytetracycline, chlortetracycline, demethylchlortetracycline and minocycline (Minocin). They all act in the same way but each one may have a slightly different strength of action on

63

different types of bacteria. Also, the speed at which the tetracyclines pass into the bloodstream may differ. Other differences are the result of their being distributed slightly differently in the various tissues of the body. Some are very cleverly made up so that although you only have to take them once or twice a day they have an action over the whole twenty-four hours. Minocycline is one of these. Local preparations are usually prescribed with the tetracycline, to increase the effectiveness of the treatment. Amongst the tetracyclines, minocycline is rather different. Most tetracyclines should be taken on an empty stomach or they may not work properly. Minocycline is not affected by food or milk so it does not matter when you take it.

Probably the antibiotic most often prescribed is tetracycline itself – one of the oldest members of this group. Treatment varies but it often starts off with one tablet, or capsule or pill, three times a day (250 mgs three times per day) and comes down to two tablets a day after a week or two. The dose is then adjusted to suit your needs. It may be as low as one tablet every other day, or, if your condition has not improved, the dose will be increased. Once or twice I have had to give people as many as eight tablets a day!

### How long do antibiotics take to work?
These antibiotics take some time to work. You will not notice an improvement for at least six weeks, and probably as long as eight to ten weeks. Something like 70 per cent of people with acne are much improved after about eight weeks of oral treatment with tetracyclines. As with all the other types, the important thing is to persist with the treatment.

You will find that your acne will continue to improve for several months, as long as you go on taking the drug. The way to test whether your acne condition has burnt itself out is to stop the tablets every so often. But let your doctor guide you in this. If the spots return after a few days you will have to continue with the tablets. Most people seem to need at least six months' treatment with tetracyclines and some have to keep on taking them for a few years.

### Side effects
The tetracyclines are one of the safest group of drugs and side effects are uncommon, even after long periods. But there are a number of possible effects, even if rare:

**Biliousness** A few people have a little indigestion or feel a bit bilious. Some doctors encourage people taking tetracyclines to eat plenty of yoghurt as it has been suggested that the bacteria in the yoghurt will help prevent any change in bowel habit caused by the drug, but the evidence for this is a little thin. Very rarely the problem of diarrhoea becomes serious, and this is then known as pseudomembranous colitis and needs to be urgently treated in hospital.

**Vaginal thrush** seems to be more common in women taking tetracyclines. This is an infection caused by a yeast-type of fungus which seems to gain the upper hand when the usual bacteria in the body are altered by antibiotic treatment. Soreness and vaginal discharge are typical of thrush and if you get these symptoms tell your doctor so that you start appropriate treatment.

**Rashes** Although it is uncommon to get a rash if you are taking tetracyclines there is one type that can occur if you have been taking the drug and have then been exposed to sunlight. Demclocycline seems prone to cause it. The rash looks like bad sunburn and can make you quite sore and uncomfortable. Your fingernails can loosen at the same time. Luckily these effects are only short-lived and full recovery rapidly takes place.

**Pregnancy** You shouldn't take the tetracyclines if there is any possibility that you may be pregnant. They may discolour and deform the developing child's teeth and can also affect the bones.

**Bacterial resistance** Unfortunately the same problems of bacterial resistance can happen with orally given antibiotics as with the local treatments. However, as I said on page 61, the chance of resistance spreading may be slightly less with an orally administered drug. In any case, the condition for which these are given is generally more severe and any risk is therefore more justifiable.

### The other antibiotics and similar drugs
There are a number of antibiotics which may be prescribed instead of tetracyclines, but it is probable that you would be given them only if your doctor had already tried you on the popular ones and there hadn't been any improvement, or if you had had some side effects.

**Erythromycin** Most of what I have said about the tetracyclines applies to erythromycin. This is the second most frequently prescribed antibiotic for acne. It is given in the same dosage and for the same period as the tetracyclines. Like the tetracyclines, erythromycin is a very safe antibiotic and is only rarely the cause of side effects.

**Ampicillin** This is another antibiotic that can be used for acne. It is related to penicillin but affects a different range of bacteria from penicillin. Its use in acne is quite similar to the tetracyclines and erythromycin. Mostly it is as safe as they are but it can sometimes cause allergic reactions. If you are sensitive to penicillin and come out in a rash when given it you should not have ampicillin as the same thing can happen.

**Clindamycin** This is an antibiotic that has been used for acne when the others haven't worked and the condition is still very inflamed and troublesome. Dermatologists who have used it for very severe acne say that it can be very helpful. Unfortunately it can cause some unpleasant side effects and is not a favourite of mine for this reason. The side effect that has made it notorious is the bad sort of bowel upset called pseudomembranous colitis. Clindamycin can also, very rarely, cause some blood disorders.

**The sulphonamides** These are not antibiotics because they are not produced by micro-organisms but are artificially manufactured. Some have been used in the treatment of acne, and one in particular called sulphamethoxy pyridazine (Lederkyn) became popular among doctors for a time. Unfortunately it can produce some very unpleasant side effects including blood disorders and nasty all-over rashes. So in my opinion it is not a good treatment for acne.

**Trimethoprim** This is another type of non-antibiotic agent which is combined with a sulphonamide in tablet form (Bactrim, Septrin). It has also been used in acne and apparently with good results. As with the sulphonamides, there can only be very few people who would have this drug prescribed rather than one of the more popular antibiotics.

### The retinoid drugs

The retinoids are derived from vitamin A (also known as retinol). Vitamin A is a vitamin found in dairy produce and liver and also in vegetables (as 'carotenes' which are converted to vitamin A in the body). We need vitamin A to grow, to reproduce, to see at night and to have healthy skin. About forty years ago some doctors tried it for skin diseases of several kinds because they knew it was necessary for healthy skin, and they found that in some cases their patients did very well. When vitamin A was given in massive doses, the acne seemed to respond. Unfortunately the large doses that were necessary for the improvement were very near the doses that produce serious toxic (poisonous) side effects. Because of this and some other doctors saying that the treatment really wasn't very good anyway, vitamin A fell out of fashion. However, the interest in it was kept alive in the pharmaceutical industry and amongst researchers. The first treatment to be made including vitamin A was retinoic acid, a local preparation (see page 59). This seemed quite effective and encouraged the production of other retinoid drugs. Now several retinoid drugs are being tested and they look very promising for many fields of medicine.

### Isotretinoin

The retinoid of most interest to us is called 13-cis retinoic acid or isotretinoin (Roaccutane). At the time of writing it has just been released for hospital use in the UK, but has had a licence in the USA for some time.

The most exciting thing to me about this drug is that it is especially helpful for very severe acne – the sort that has been quite difficult to

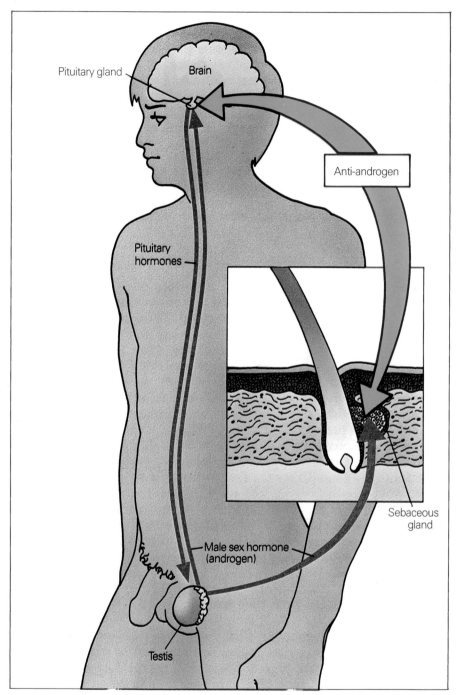

Pituitary gland

Brain

Anti-androgen

Pituitary
hormones

Sebaceous
gland

Male sex hormone
(androgen)

Testis

Anti-androgens work by stopping greasiness of the skin developing.

improve. Most of the clinical research on isotretinoin has been done in the USA, in Germany and in the UK, and all the reports have been very enthusiastic. About 80 per cent of patients with severe cystic acne are much improved after only four months' treatment. A quite fascinating thing about the drug is that improvement continues even after you have stopped taking it and the improvement is maintained in many people, so to all intents and purposes the condition is cured. Only a very small number require a second course of treatment. Isotretinoin seems to work in three ways:

- By making the sebaceous glands secrete much less sebum, with the glands themselves becoming quite dramatically smaller

- Possibly by loosening the blackheads and so unblocking the hair follicles.

- By suppressing inflammation.

**Side effects** No drug is entirely free from side effects, and as might be expected, this one has its share. Luckily in most cases they are tolerable and do not mean treatment has to be stopped. The commonest one is slight peeling and dryness of the lips – this happens to virtually everyone taking the drug. About 20 per cent of people taking it lose hair from their scalp at a mildly increased rate only while they are taking it and some find that their skin becomes slightly peely, especially on the palms and soles, and generally more itchy. It can also increase the fat in the blood. If you are normal to start with, this should not be a problem as the drug is only taken for a short period.

The only potentially very serious problem is that isotretinoin can cause deformities in babies born to mothers taking it. For this reason it is very important that women taking the drug understand the need to take effective contraceptive precautions. It has no effect on a man's sperm, so there would be no danger to a child fathered by a man taking the drug.

I have no doubt that the development of this drug is the start of an entirely new era in the treatment of acne. Other, similar but even more effective and less toxic drugs will almost certainly follow in the not too distant future.

### Hormone treatments – how they work in acne

**Anti-androgens** Remembering what I said about the way androgens (the male sex hormones) stimulate sebum secretion and so play an important part in causing acne (see page 16), you will not be surprised that drugs opposing the actions of androgens have been tried in the treatment of acne. They are known as anti-androgens and they can be given either by mouth or locally.

There are several powerful anti-androgens, and the problem has been to develop drugs that have an action on the sebaceous glands but don't stop androgens working elsewhere in the body. The androgens have many important functions apart from stimulating sebum secretion – not least of them is that they are responsible for the sex drive. In fact it is better to give this type of drug locally rather than by mouth, as in this way the anti-androgen effect occurs on the skin, with its sebaceous glands, rather than in the whole body. Unfortunately it has proved rather difficult to make a preparation that goes deep enough into the skin to affect the sebaceous glands and still not have effects elsewhere in the body.

**Oestrogens** The anti-androgen type of treatment was tried many years ago, before proper anti-androgen compounds were available. Oestrogens (the female sex hormones) have much the same effect in drying up sebum secretion and they were used sometimes when no other treatments seemed to work. The oestrogens are still used by some doctors for women with bad acne – though I don't think they are ever given to men.

When oestrogens are prescribed for young women their periods may be altered. The bleeding may last a shorter time or it may not happen at all. For this reason some doctors prefer to prescribe the oestrogen tablets for, say, three weeks at a time and then allow one week off.

**Combined preparations** There is one tablet that can be prescribed in the UK that contains both an anti-androgen and an oestrogen (Diane). It contains cyproterone acetate (the anti-androgen) and ethinyloestradiol (the oestrogen). As with the other hormone drugs of this type it is recommended that it is given for three weeks at a time with a week's rest between courses. While being taken it acts as a contraceptive pill. It effectively opposes the androgen action on the sebaceous glands and even stops the production of androgens in the body. It is based on a sound scientific principle and there have been some encouraging reports of the effects of this drug in acne.

**Side effects** Of course there are some side effects – as you may expect with a hormone preparation. They are mainly like those experienced by women on the Pill:

- Slight nausea, headache and fatigue

- There may be some irregularities of the periods, but these are generally not too troublesome

- Migraine may be caused by the drug, though this is fairly uncommon

- Although the evidence is not clear there seems to be a possibility of abnormalities developing in unborn children if the drug is taken during pregnancy. If there is any doubt as to whether you are pregnant or not you must tell your doctor so that he or she knows not to give you the drug.

There is another problem with these anti-androgens, or Pill-type hormone preparations. You may have heard the question debated on television in relation to the Pill, or seen some discussion of it in newspapers or magazines. This concerns thrombosis, a clotting of the blood. Thrombosis can affect anyone but it is more likely in people who are overweight and those who smoke. The thrombosis can be trivial or very serious if it affects the blood vessels of the brain. It is thought that there is some slight increased risk of thrombosis developing in women taking the Pill, particularly those who are overweight or smoke, and the same may be true of anti-androgens. However, you must view the matter in proportion – the risk of developing a thrombosis while taking these drugs is about the same as if you were pregnant.

## Anti-inflammatory drugs – corticosteroids
In theory, using these drugs in acne should 'damp down' the inflammation and so also aid the acne. Curiously this approach has not been very

Surgical treatment can be successful for people with persistent and severe acne.

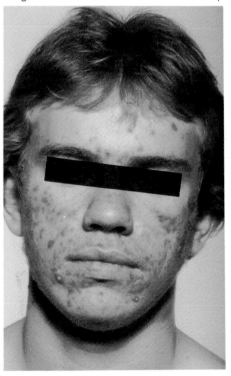 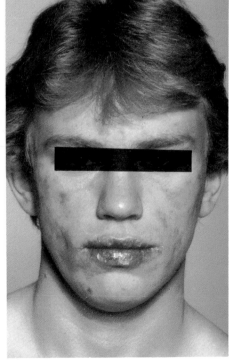

successful as yet. The corticosteroids (cortisone-like drugs) certainly are anti-inflammatory but are only given infrequently in tablet form for acne (although I describe on page 62 how cortisone can be combined in a local treatment). I suppose most doctors would think giving these powerful drugs for acne overly heavy handed. 'About as appropriate as using a Centurion tank to swat a fly,' I heard one doctor say. All the same, I believe that in some rare acne cases corticosteroids may be used, but it would only be for very severely affected people who could develop unpleasant scars that this form of treatment would be considered.

**Side effects**  There are many side effects of these drugs – too many to talk about all of them here. But if I say that they can cause gastric ulcers, diabetes, high blood pressure and even acne, that should be sufficient! This is why treatment with them has to be carefully regulated.

# Surgical treatments for acne

There are surgical treatments for acne of all degrees:

- Routine surgical methods for treating cysts and large, ugly scars

- Plastic surgical techniques for dealing with the shallow pockmarks and pits left after the spots themselves have gone

- Minor surgery (if you can call it that) to remove blackheads and pustules.

### Routine surgery
This is more popular with surgeons than with dermatologists. Most dermatologists are very hesitant to advise surgical treatment for cysts, even when it seems that they are ready to discharge. The reasons for this are that the fluid inside the cyst often accumulates again anyway, and that the surgery can sometimes result in an unpleasant scar. There are anyway better treatments for the cysts using drugs or other techniques.

So far as large and ugly scars are concerned, surgery is not often very successful in removing these permanently and some other type of treatment is necessary as well. Sometimes X-ray treatment is given after surgery and sometimes steroids are injected into the areas as well.

### Plastic surgery and 'minor surgery'
When there is shallow pock and pit scarring, some doctors have attempted to flatten the skin using a rotating wire brush. This is known as dermabrasion. It is less painful than it sounds, but you can expect some soreness that will last for a few days. This method cannot be used if you still have

any active acne spots and it does not give a good result, cosmetically speaking, in dark-skinned people. This is because it can sometimes cause changes in the skin's pigment. Dermabrasion was quite fashionable at one time but is now only practised in a few centres.

Peeling the skin with an acid solution has been tried by some doctors and they say this can also help superficial scarring. It is not something that I would advise without being persuaded by more evidence.

## X-ray treatment

There was a fashion up to about fifteen years ago for treating acne with a special kind of X-ray. Not many dermatologists use this type of treatment now – it certainly did not seem to be very effective when put to the test.

## Cryotherapy

This means treatment by freezing. Some large acne cysts seem to clear up with a particular type of freezing treatment using either a stick of solid carbon dioxide or a special instrument with has a probe tip cooled with liquid nitrogen gas. You may have seen a similar treatment for warts. Cryotherapy can be painful but it appears to be able to flatten off particularly unpleasant cysts.

In the next chapter you can read about the uncommon and severe types of acne for which some of these new medical treatments have been used.

# 6 SPECIAL TYPES OF ACNE

So far I have described the ordinary acne that affects most people to some degree. In this chapter I go into the uncommon types of acne and the very severe forms. I also describe some skin conditions that are often mistaken for acne because they resemble it so closely.

## Uncommon types of acne

### Infantile acne
Acne is thought of as a disease of teenagers but it can affect other age groups as well. It often comes as a surprise to my students that acne can affect young children and even infants a few months old. Of course, acne in infancy is quite uncommon. To give some idea of how unusual it is the average dermatologist may only see four or five affected children in a year.

Blackheads, small papules and pustules develop over the cheeks mainly but some spots may also develop on the forehead and chin. They don't seem to occur over the chest, back or shoulders. Luckily larger acne spots don't appear in infantile acne and scarring doesn't follow the smaller papules and pustules.

We really don't have much of an idea why acne descends on these children. They are usually fit in all other respects. But there is one very rare exception. This is when there are more androgens (see page 16) in the blood than there should be, and then the acne that develops may be quite severe and there are usually other abnormalities as well.

Infantile acne can last for an annoyingly long time but it does eventually fade away. The affected children don't seem to be very distressed about their spots – but naturally their parents are and I find that they need a lot of support and reassurance.

Treatment is the same as for anyone with acne, except that children usually only need very mild treatments with the weakest of creams and lotions.

Children who have had acne do not seem more likely to develop severe acne as teenagers than anyone else.

### Acne in old age
Every so often I will see an elderly person in my clinic who, for no very obvious reason, suddenly develops a crop of acne spots. When this happens

73

we have to be careful before we start treatment to see whether there is a special underlying reason for the acne. Some medicines including steroid drugs such as corticosteroids can make acne develop (see page 77) or, as in infants, it may be the result of there being too many androgens in the blood.

**Blackheads**

Blackheads usually mean acne, however mild – but not always. They sometimes appear without any other spots or blemishes. In the elderly, for example, blackheads are sometimes seen on the upper parts of the cheeks and around the eyes. This seems to happen when people have had a great deal of exposure to the sun in the past, and these so-called senile comedones are usually found alongside wrinkling of the skin caused by the sun. If treatment is required the blackheads can be removed with a blackhead extractor (see page 45).

Occasionally one solitary very large blackhead forms on the trunk of the body. This should be easily recognized as the blackened greasy plug appears in the middle of a dimple. Some of these giant comedones become so large that they are mistaken for tumours of the skin!

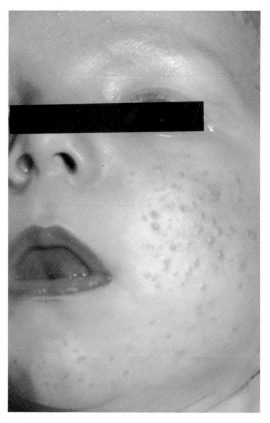

A baby with acne – a very unusual case.

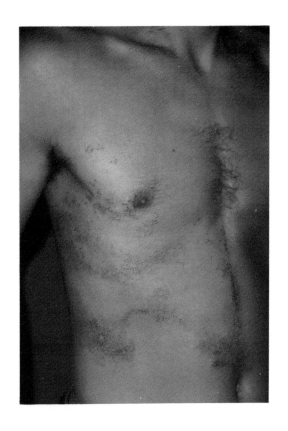

A large crop of blackheads, known as comedone naevus.

## Comedone naevus

Naevus is a medical name for birthmark and a comedone naevus is not really proper acne at all, but for completeness it is worth including here. Comedone naevus is quite rare, and is really a type of birthmark. Many blackheads appear on one area of skin – which may be anywhere. Sometimes inflamed spots develop as well but this is unusual. The abnormality is probably congenital (that is, there is an abnormality in the way the skin is formed) so that the way the horn forms in some follicles makes blackheads particularly likely to develop in that area.

## Occupational acne

Some people are unlucky enough to develop bad acne because of the conditions where they work. In Chapter 2 I talked about different sorts of sweaty and oily jobs which can cause mild acne in anyone. But this can become quite serious in some circumstances. Perhaps the simplest to understand is the quite severe acne experienced by soldiers in the Far East. After being on active service in hot and humid climates some of them flared up with unpleasant acne. The individual spots tended to be very large and quite inflamed. As their skin became very moist from sweat and they were living in the relatively unhygienic conditions of war their hair follicles would have become blocked, which led on to the bad acne. When these soldiers were transferred to a cooler climate the acne calmed down again.

**Chloracne** The most severe type of occupational acne occurs in workers exposed to chemicals such as the chlorinated hydrocarbons and dioxin. It is known as chloracne and it is a most unpleasant disorder.

The chemicals responsible cause the acne after being absorbed into the body in some way – they do not have to come in contact with the skin surface, as with oils and grease.

Large inflamed acne spots and cysts occur all over the body and last for a long time. They may continue to erupt for many months after exposure to the chemicals has ended.

Usually great care is taken to protect workers in chemical plants where the toxic materials are made. Unfortunately accidents do happen and only minute traces are necessary to cause chloracne. Such accidents have happened several times in the recent past, the most famous being the Seveso disaster near Milan in Italy. Here an explosion at a chemical plant resulted in contamination of a large area with the chemical Dioxin and caused many cases of chloracne in the local community.

Soldiers in hot, tropical climates develop acne fairly often.

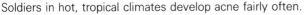

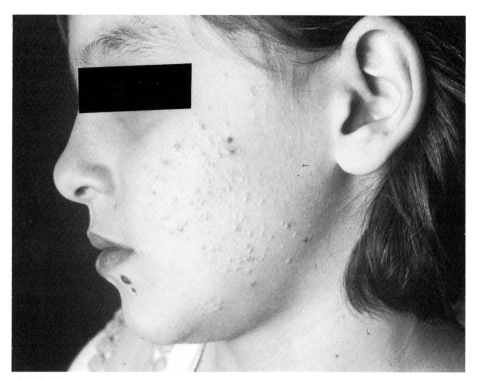

A child from Seveso, Italy with chloracne.

## Acne caused by drugs

**Steroids** There are some drugs which have the unfortunate side effect of causing acne. Probably the commonest type of drug-caused acne is due to steroid-type drugs. These are sometimes given for arthritis and for other chronic diseases, so they can be responsible for acne in old age. Steroid drugs are usually given for quite long periods and steroid acne usually doesn't occur until the tablets have been taken for some weeks. When it does develop there are often other, more serious side effects. This type of acne is not usually severe. The spots tend to be numerous but small and not very inflamed.

Acne can also develop after steroid-containing creams have been applied to the skin. This mainly happens after the cream has been covered with an air-tight dressing so that it is held in contact with the skin for some days.

**Hormone treatment** We have already seen that sebum secretion is controlled by androgens (see page 16). Sometimes doctors have to prescribe androgen-type hormone treatment for other disorders, either by pill or by injection. When this happens there is a possibility of acne developing – and then the acne is just like ordinary acne.

**Drug treatments for epilepsy and tuberculosis** Acne can break out after other types of drug treatment but we are not certain about the relationship with many of the drugs blamed. Some of the drugs used to treat epilepsy, for example, are said to cause acne – particularly drugs like Epanutin; and one of the drugs used to treat tuberculosis, called Isoniazid, is also thought to make acne spots appear. If these drugs really do cause acne the way they do so is quite mysterious.

**Treatment**
When it is certain that the drug with which you are being treated is causing the acne, your doctor will change your prescription and the spots should disappear. If they are persistent he will try one of the acne treatments I described in Chapter 5.

# Severe types and complications of acne

### Cystic acne
This is the worst kind of acne. Happily the condition is fairly uncommon. I don't suppose that I see more than about eight or ten people a year with cystic acne – and most of them have a mild attack. Although rare in anybody, it is more often seen in young men than in girls. Usually it comes on in people who have had acne for some time. The condition suddenly worsens for no known reason, with large cysts appearing. The number of cysts varies from just one or two to more than twenty. They range from about the size of a grape to that of a plum. As might be expected, there are lots of ordinary acne spots present as well as the cysts.

Cystic acne can be a painful disorder and can make people feel unwell. Indeed, some people I have seen with bad cystic acne have needed a few days' care and attention in hospital.

**Treatment** Cystic acne may calm down as quickly as it erupted, though it can also grumble on for quite some time. The condition responds well to treatment and if you begin to develop cysts you should not hesitate to see a specialist. This is very important as most dermatologists experienced in treating severe forms of acne say that early treatments can reduce the chances of scarring – and unpleasant hypertrophic or keloid scars (see page 19) can follow cystic acne, particularly over the neck, shoulders and chest.

Large and very painful cysts started to appear quite unexpectedly over Jack's neck, jaw and back in the space of three or four weeks. He had had mild acne previously and had used a cream containing sulphur that the local pharmacist had sold him. His doctor was alarmed by the appearance of the cysts and arranged an appointment with a dermatologist. This doctor recognized that Jack had a rare and severe type of acne and organized his admission into hospital. At one time treatment for this rare type of resistant cystic acne was lengthy and difficult but luckily the situation has changed. Jack was given the new retinoid drug 13-cis retinoic acid and after about ten weeks most of the cysts had flattened and were rapidly disappearing, and no new ones appeared.

## Acne fulminans
This condition is a very severe and rare variety of cystic acne (I have only seen four people with it). People who have it will be miserable and uncomfortable because of the painful cysts and they may also feel ill for two other reasons: they can develop mild fever; and they may suffer from inflamed and painful joints (the condition known as arthritis). The reason for the fever and arthritis is unknown but they may indicate that the body's immune system is reacting to the severe acne.

**Treatment** People with this condition need to be admitted to hospital,

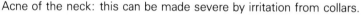

Acne of the neck: this can be made severe by irritation from collars.

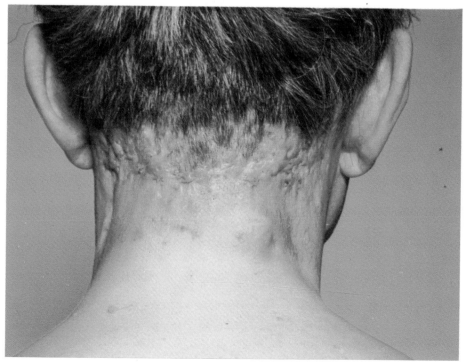

79

where they may require treatment with corticosteroids, which damp down the inflammatory reaction (see page 62).

## Cystic acne of the neck

Another variety of cystic acne that is sometimes seen and is perhaps not quite so uncommon as acne fulminans is known as sycosis nuchae. It occurs in young men mainly and may be made worse by continual fiddling with the skin in this region. In this condition large, inflamed spots and cysts form on the back of the neck and cause prominent scarring. Its treatment is as for ordinary acne.

## Acne of the scalp

Acne is a disease of the hair follicles and so anywhere there is hair it may develop. For this reason it may seem odd that the scalp is so rarely involved. One explanation for this is the large hairs in the scalp hair follicles allow the sebum to drain away and so keep them from being blocked. However, the scalp is very occasionally affected. It takes several forms:

1. Inflamed spots form and then crust over, to leave scars

2. Progressive and destructive acne causes loss of hair and scarring

3. One type of bacteria of the skin grows out of proportion to the others and causes pustules; in this acne pustules are the only spots that develop.

The second and third types I have described are extremely uncommon.

**Treatment** Acne of the scalp is treated with antibiotics that attack the bacteria causing the spots.

A similar type of acne to 3 described above has been recorded elsewhere on the skin. This is due to treatment with antibiotic tablets for long periods. An invading bacteria grows in the hair follicles and causes pus spots. Normally the skin's own bacteria prevent this from happening but after antibiotic treatment they are decreased in numbers. Only bacteria that themselves are not affected by the antibiotics given for acne can do this.

## Acne of the armpits and groin

There is an uncommon disorder that affects the skin of the armpits and groin and is known by the terrifying name of hidradenitis suppurativa. Although it is, strictly speaking, not acne, it is an inflamed condition of the special hair follicles and sweat glands found in these regions and is considered by many dermatologists to be part of the acne picture. It occurs in both sexes a little later in life than ordinary acne, but is also sometimes seen in people in their late teens and early twenties. It sometimes develops alongside severe ordinary acne.

In the armpits and groin there are special sweat glands known as the apocrine glands. Unlike the sweat glands over the rest of the body surface they don't open independently on to the skin surface but into the hair follicles, and they do not make a watery kind of sweat but a thick, viscid type. At one time in the development of the human race these glands may have been concerned with attraction of the other sex by smell.

In this acne condition inflamed spots form which break down and discharge when they reach a large enough size. In a very few unfortunate people large, discharging spots continue to form and make life very difficult because of the pain and discomfort that they cause.

**Treatment** for this condition varies according to how severe it is. For the mildest type an antiseptic lotion dabbed on the affected areas twice daily is sufficient. When there are spots, antibiotics are often prescribed in the same way as for ordinary acne. In my experience they are not as effective as for ordinary acne and something else will probably be required. Newer drugs may help some people – in particular the retinoid drug 13-cis retinoic acid (see page 66).

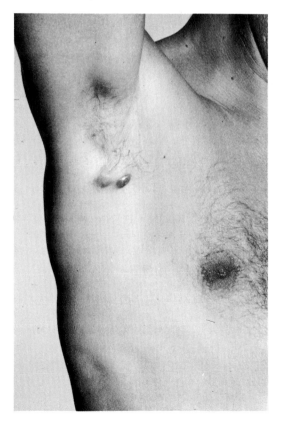

In this condition called hidradenitis suppurativa, acne-like spots appear in the armpits or groin.

Some doctors recommend an operation to remove most of the hair follicles of the affected regions but this should only be necessary for the most severe cases.

# Conditions that mimic acne

Several skin diseases have inflamed acne-type spots but aren't really acne. It's important that you should know that there are other, similar-looking disorders as you may not have acne but another condition that needs different treatment.

### Rosacea

One skin disease that is sometimes mistaken for acne is a condition of the face known as rosacea. To make matters more confusing some doctors call it acne rosacea – even though it has little to do with ordinary acne.

Acne-type papules do occur in rosacea but they are not tender as in acne and when they are present other blemishes are always there as well. These points should help you identify the condition:

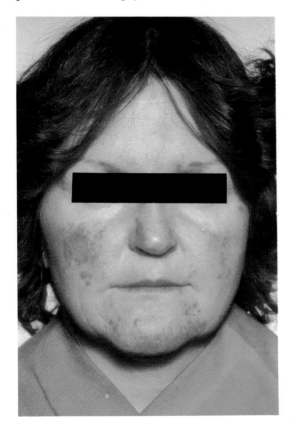

Rosacea: the inflammation makes the condition look like acne, though it is entirely different.

- The skin of the cheeks, nose, forehead and chin is red and often has little worm-like veins on the surface (telangiectasia)

- The skin is not usually as greasy in rosacea as in acne and there are not usually many blackheads

- The rash appears mainly on the face, although sometimes the neck too is affected

- Spots hardly ever appear on the shoulders, back or chest.

**Treatment** Rosacea responds quite well to the antibiotic tetracycline when given by mouth. It also responds to erythromycin and another non-antibiotic antibacterial drug called metronidazole. In fact it is cleared much more quickly by these drugs than acne is, and local treatments aren't necessary.

Although the spots go quickly (in about six weeks), the red colour of the skin takes much longer to calm down.

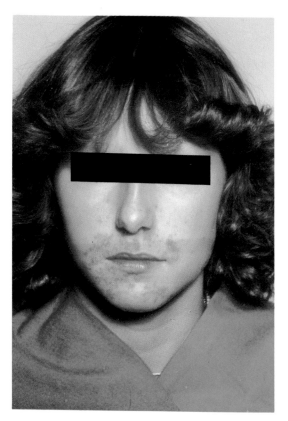

Perioral dermatitis – another skin condition like acne but needing different treatment.

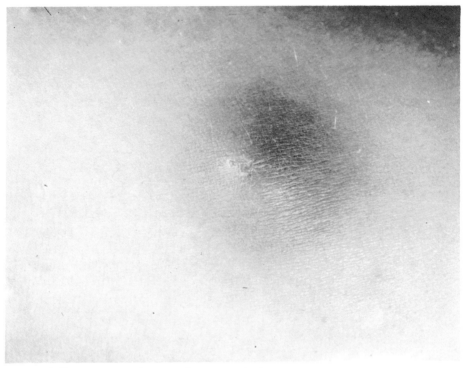
Boils look like acne cysts but usually appear singly.

**Perioral dermatitis**
Small papules and pus spots also occur in the condition known as perioral dermatitis. The spots develop around the mouth and at the side of the nose and are generally smaller but more numerous than in acne.

Oddly enough perioral dermatitis is virtually restricted to young women. Even more surprising is the fact that it was almost unknown before the middle of the 1960s. It has been suggested that its sudden appearance was related to the use of creams that contain corticosteroids. Because spots develop in perioral dermatitis it is sometimes mistaken for acne but really it shouldn't be as it has a quite different appearance.

**Treatment** As with rosacea, this is based on oral treatment with tetracycline. The condition responds completely in about three or four weeks. It is important that no steroid creams are given.

**Eczema**
This causes scaling and itchiness – neither of which is typical for acne. Sometimes a special variety of eczema known as seborrhoeic eczema can be slightly lumpy and does break out in the acne areas. But it is still scaly

84

like other eczemas and really doesn't look like acne.

## Boils and other spots

Boils can be mistaken for acne spots, as the spots are red and may develop pus in their centres. There are several features which distinguish them from acne spots:

1. Usually they are a brighter red and are painful and more tender

2. They are few in number, occur on any hairy part of the body and are not accompanied by other signs of acne.

Some of you will say, 'Aren't acne papules the same kind of thing as boils anyway?' The answer to this is most definitely 'No!' Boils are the result of an infection of the skin by virulent bacteria and acne spots are not. The virulent bacteria (usually a micro-organism called Staphylococcus aureus) gain entry into the skin through a hair follicle and do their dirty work in the follicle. The destruction of tissue by the bacteria and the skin's reaction cause the pus often seen in a boil. When a boil gets very large or several boils join together the big, lumpish boil that results is called a carbuncle.

Formation of a boil.

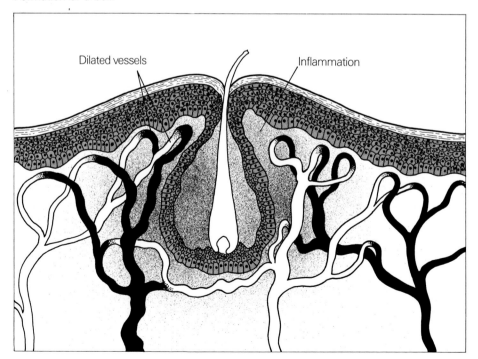

**Treatment** Because boils are painful and can spread you should have them medically treated. Depending on how bad they are, your doctor will probably either prescribe an antibiotic cream, or if they persist and come to a head he may recommend that you have them lanced to release the pus. As there is no widespread inflammation you should not be bothered with any scarring after the boils have gone.

## Shaving rash
Another mild infection of the hair follicles by bacteria causes a lot of small papules and pustules to occur in the beard areas on the neck and face of men. It can be caused by shaving and will be cleared up with an antiseptic cream.

This rash can be quite difficult to tell apart from acne and is called folliculitis.

Although some of these skin conditions sound very unpleasant and anybody unlucky enough to get one of the severe forms will suffer quite a lot of discomfort, we are now able to improve all of them considerably with drug treatments – as you have seen in this and the last chapter. In Chapter 7 I show what is being done and what still needs to be done in the way of research to make these treatments quicker and even more effective.

# 7 RESEARCH IN ACNE

Both people with acne and their parents often ask me about the latest research into acne. Since it is still such a common skin disorder and we still do not have a rapid and trouble-free cure it is obvious that more research is necessary. However, a great deal has been learnt in the past twenty years, especially about sebaceous secretion and its control. There has also been a lot of investigation into the part played by the skin's bacteria in the causes of acne. In this chapter I will summarize what is being done on these and other important features of acne, and in what areas further work is necessary.

## Sebum secretion

**Measuring the rate of secretion** In Chapter 1 I described how seborrhoea has a fundamental role in the development of acne. Some researchers think sebum secretion so important that they have devised ways of measuring its rate. There are two methods. The first depends on the way grease soaks into paper. The most common area of skin to be investigated in this way is the forehead, but centres of the back or the chest are sometimes also measured. All the grease on the surface of the skin is cleaned off. Then very clean cigarette papers are first weighed and then held in close contact with the skin surface by an adhesive plaster or by a strap of some kind. They are left there for about two hours and then weighed again. As the area of skin being investigated is known, it is possible to work out the weight (in mgs) of sebum secretion by the skin per $cm^2$ (unit area) per hour.

The second method used is a fairly new one and it is simpler and quicker, but it relies on complex instruments. The area of skin is first cleaned and then the grease that develops is picked up by a special crystal which is pressed on to the skin. The crystal is measured in a special instrument and the changes in it are recorded electrically.

These techniques are still mainly used in research but the day may well come when the type of treatment you receive for your acne will depend on how fast your skin makes sebum.

## Hormones
It is now generally agreed that androgens are important in causing seborrhoea (see Chapter 1), but it is only comparatively recently that very

sensitive and accurate methods for measuring androgens in the blood have been available. They have shown that people with acne frequently have slightly raised levels of the androgen testosterone in the blood. We now need to know exactly how this affects the development of acne – including the way androgens act on the chemistry of the hair follicles and change either the rate of sebum secretion or the way the horn is formed, or both. Such knowledge could help in the development of drugs that would suppress sebum secretion by interfering with the action of the hormones on the oil glands and other cells in the hair follicles.

In contrast there is a theory that instead of there being increased concentrations of androgens in the blood, the sebaceous glands are more sensitive to a normal level of androgens. That is, more sebum is made by the glands for a normal level of testosterone. Testosterone and other androgens undergo a complex series of chemical reactions before the sebaceous gland cells are 'turned on' to secrete sebum. It seems quite possible that there is a difference in the way that the sebaceous glands in the skin of acne sufferers chemically change the sex hormones. Anyway, as you can see, more research is required to sort out exactly what is happening.

An important part of research in acne: measuring the rate of sebum secretion.

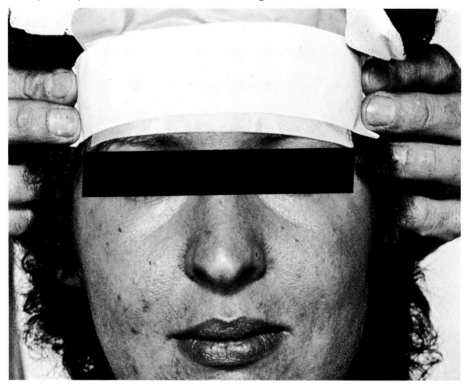

## The forming of blackheads

As I explained in Chapter 1, it has been suspected by dermatologists that the way surface horn is formed in hair follicles with blackheads is different from normal. It may be that fatty acids produced in the hair follicle irritate the delicate lining, causing this different horn to form. The horn produced in this way seems to be very sticky and does not easily leave the hair follicle, making an obstruction. Once this obstruction occurs the scene is set for inflammation. This is an important area for research as, if we could definitely uncover what causes the stickiness or this horn, which makes the blockage, we could begin to design treatments to stop the follicles blocking.

## Bacteria and antibiotics

In Chapter 1 I described how the bacteria normally present on the skin's surface and in the hair follicles may be splitting the fats in sebum and liberating the fatty acids that I have just talked about. Even if this is so, we need to know much more about the details of the process. Are all the bacteria on the skin responsible for this or just some of them? Another important question that continually pops up concerns the way that antibiotics work. Do these drugs act by cutting down the numbers of bacteria and so lessen the splitting of the fats in sebum, or do they have some other action? Research hasn't given us the answers yet but clearly this question is of great importance in deciding on the development of new antibacterial treatments for acne.

## Inflammation

Another important aspect of acne that needs much more study is the inflammation that accompanies the disorder. After all, it is the inflammation that causes most of the features that we recognize as acne. I find it surprising that comparatively little is known about how or why this inflammation develops. It seems that the contents of hair follicles blocked with blackheads leak into the surrounding skin (see Chapter 1). But is it the hair or the horn, the sebum or the bacteria, or combinations of all these materials, that produce the inflammation?

Besides these factors, some researchers think that the body's immune system may play a part in the inflammation in acne. They claim that people with acne have immunological abnormalities and that these may contribute to the development of the inflammation.

Research into inflammation in general has become quite sophisticated and it is likely that there will soon be drugs produced that can attack it at its different stages. It is therefore particularly important that we learn more about the causes of acne inflammation so that the most appropriate anti-inflammatory drugs can be tried in the disease. For example, if we could discover why large numbers of white cells accumulate in some areas we could stop acne cysts from forming with suitable drugs.

**Scar formation** is a bit of a mystery and we need more information on why some people form scars and others don't. It would also be helpful to know what it is about acne that makes scars appear. Then of course there should by very much more research on the treatment of acne scars.

## The need for social and environmental research
Apart from the clinical research there are other areas that should be studied to help combat acne. We still don't know much about the extent to which acne occurs in different racial groups, in different social groups and at various times of life. It is true that we have a broad general picture but there are still too many gaps. As I said in Chapter 2, it is now not generally believed that diet makes any difference either to the development or cure of acne. All the same, differences in diet in different communities over many years may be a contributory factor in the occurrence of acne in different races and groups – at least that is the opinion of one group of researchers. For this reason it would be helpful to study eating habits in different groups of people over several years and correlate the findings with the amount and type of acne that the various groups get.

## New treatments
Another sort of research that is perhaps not quite so exciting, but in many ways just as important, is the trial of new treatments for acne. We always need to know whether this, that or the other treatment is better than, worse than or as good as, another treatment. These trials are necessary to develop the most efficient treatments with the fewest side effects. Sometimes they are conducted in what is called a double blind trial. This means that to avoid unconscious bias, neither the person with acne nor the doctor knows whether the treatment being tested or the treatment to which it is being compared is being taken. Permission has to be obtained from everyone who enters such a trial, and there should be no pressure on anyone who doesn't want to. If you are ever asked to take part in this type of clinical trial I hope that you will agree, because it is only in this way that we can decide which treatments are worthwhile.

## Looking to the future
It may seem that any advance in our understanding of acne is likely to arise quite by chance in the course of some other investigation. There is no denying that many major breakthroughs in medicine have come from unexpected sources and it is quite possible this may happen in acne.

It is also possible that important knowledge about acne will come from another area of research, for example, from research into the general mechanisms of inflammation, which appears in many other disorders besides acne.

Even though these possibilities exist, it would be wrong just to sit back and wait for them to happen. I believe that we need an active programme

Enjoy friends' company and you'll forget your acne worries.

of research in acne and I think that it is sad that compared to many other common disorders there is so little. The reason for this, as in many areas of medicine, is quite simply lack of resources: dermatological research doesn't command much public sympathy.

Despite this gloomy note, I am very hopeful that many of the mysteries surrounding acne will be solved in the next ten or twenty years and treatments will be improved in the same period.

# 8 QUESTIONS AND ANSWERS

People I see with acne often ask me about how acne develops and whether the sort of conditions they think make it worse really do affect their spots. As you will have seen from reading this book, there are no short answers that explain these things fully, but I have listed here some of the questions I am most frequently asked with brief answers that I hope you will find useful as a quick reference.

**Why have I developed acne?**
Because you are no different from the majority of normal people. Probably everyone develops some acne at some time. Why some people's acne is worse than others' is a much more difficult question and one that we can't completely answer.

**What are acne spots?**
Acne spots are inflamed areas of skin that start in blocked hair follicles. When the inflammation is very bad the spot may become quite large and form pus at its centre – then it is known as an acne cyst.

**What is a blackhead?**
A blackhead is a plug of skin surface horn with a dark tip inside a hair follicle canal. It is the basic problem in acne as all the other inflamed spots start in a hair follicle blocked by a blackhead of some sort.

**How do acne spots form?**
Acne spots form around blocked hair follicles. They don't occur on the scalp because the hair follicles on the scalp contain a strong hair that keeps the canal open. When a fair follicle develops a blackhead, it becomes blocked. Eventually the contents of the follicle leak out into the surrounding skin and cause inflammation.

**Will my acne leave scars?**
Some scars are left after bad acne but the earlier you have treatment the less scarring you will have. If you do get some scars remember two things: there are treatments for them, and most slowly fade anyway.

**Does it matter that I pick my acne?**
This is a difficult one to answer. Mostly it doesn't matter, but if you fiddle

all the time I think that you can make matters worse. It is best to leave the spots alone if you possibly can.

## When will my acne go?
It is very easy for parents and friends (and doctors!) to say that you shouldn't worry because your teenage spots will clear up by the time you are twenty-five. It's not much comfort when you are eighteen and want to look your best. Certainly the large majority of people with acne are cleared of their spots by the time they reach their mid-twenties, but not all stop having acne then. Sometimes the condition grumbles on for a few years more.

## Will my boyfriend/girlfriend catch my acne?
No. Friends may develop acne themselves but they can't catch your acne. Acne spots are not infectious or contagious or else dermatologists would have them all the time!

## Does acne run in families?
Not as far as we know. But as everyone gets some acne it is very difficult to work out the real answer.

## Does having acne mean that you are unhealthy or run down?
No, but it can't do any harm to take things easy for a time and avoid overdoing it.

## Do nerves cause acne?
No. Being anxious or depressed sometimes makes acne worse, for example, before an exam, but does not cause acne.

## Can some drugs cause acne?
Yes. Some drugs when given by mouth can cause acne – particularly cortisone-like drugs and male sex hormones (testosterone). If you have been given a medical treatment for another condition and are worried that it may cause acne, discuss it with your doctor.

## Does the weather affect acne?
The weather does influence acne to some extent. Acne tends to improve in the summertime and this may be due to the effects of sun on the skin. It can also get worse if it is very hot and humid, and if you sweat a great deal and your skin becomes soggy, this can cause acne to worsen.

## Does washing affect acne?
Washing has only a slight effect. You can't wash acne away, but regular washing with an antibacterial preparation can help a little. Probably it's better not to alter the way you wash.

### Will my job make the acne worse?
It may. Hot, sweaty jobs tend to make acne worse. If you come into contact with oil or grease, for example, as a mechanic, this can also make acne worse. If you are a sales assistant or secretary in a company where you are asked to wear cosmetics, make sure they agree with your skin. Some don't and can make your spots worse.

### Do cosmetics affect acne?
Some thick greasy cosmetics can make acne worse and some can even bring on acne. The only way is to try different cosmetics yourself, as some will be all right for your skin and some will not agree with it. A few creams are designed to help the acne and are 'cosmetic' – so that they disguise the spots.

### Does sex affect acne?
Male sex hormone (testosterone) is very important in the development of acne. It is the hormone that stimulates the forming of grease in the skin in both men and women. As far as we know though, sexual activity doesn't bring on acne or make it worse – or better!

### Does what I eat affect my acne?
Although many people believe that sweets, chocolates and fatty foods cause acne or make it worse, experiments show that this is not true. There is not the slightest evidence that foods of any kind have any effect, good or bad.

### Is it normal to get depressed about having acne?
Nobody enjoys looking spotty and unless you are made of stern stuff it is very common to feel 'down' about your complexion sometimes. If your spots persist then you may feel very fed up and become depressed. If this happens tell your parents and if after a bit you are still upset, talk it over with your doctor.

### Will treatment from the doctor help clear my spots?
Yes, treatment will usually help your acne if you persist with it. There are many types of treatment – creams and lotions, antibiotic pills – and one of these is bound to suit you.

### Can I get some help from the pharmacy?
There are useful creams and lotions that you can buy over the counter at the pharmacy. Check with the pharmacist that they are suitable, and whether they have side effects. The more expensive items aren't necessarily the best. Preparations containing 'natural products' such as herbs or flower extracts are not usually effective.

### Should I go to my doctor about my spots?
You may need to see your doctor for the following reasons:

1. Your spots are very troublesome as there are many of them and they are painful;
2. You have tried various creams and lotions from the pharmacy and the spots refuse to go;
3. The acne spots make you feel very depressed.

## Will sunbeds help acne?
Although the sun can improve acne and some types of artificial sunlight are recommended by doctors, sunbeds are not. They may have unpleasant effects on your skin in the long term and have not been shown to help acne spots.

## Can other skin conditions look like acne?
Yes, there are several skin conditions that can look like acne. Boils and rosacea are two examples. If you have any doubt you must see your doctor who will be able to sort out the problem.

## Is there any research into acne?
Yes. There is quite a lot of research into acne – into its causes and treatment. There is research particularly on the oil secretion from the skin (sebum) and into the way the blackheads form. Treatments are improving all the time because of research.

# INTERNATIONAL DRUG NAME EQUIVALENTS

## Key
* indicates that the product contains active ingredients other than those listed.

## Note
One manufacturer's product cannot always be equated with another's owing to variations in make-up and dosage.

## Great Britain    Australia

| Generic name | Trade Name | Trade Name |
|---|---|---|
| ampicillin | Penbritin; Amfipen; Vidopen; etc. | Penbritin; Ampicyn; etc. |
| benzoyl peroxide | Acetoxyl gel; Panoxyl; Benoxyl; Debroxide; Theraderm; Quinoderm* | Benoxyl; Panoxyl; Acnayl |
| chloramphenicol | Chloromycetin; Kemicetine | Chloromycetin |
| chlortetracycline | Aureomycin | Aureomycin |
| clindamycin | Dalacin C | Dalacin C |
| cyproterone acetate + ethinyloestradiol } | Diane | not available |
| demeclocyline | Ledermycin | Ledermycin |
| erythromycin | Erythrocin; Ilosone; Arpimycin; etc. | Erythrocin; E-Mycin; Ilosone; etc. |
| ethyl lactate + zinc sulphate } | Tri-ac | not available |
| hexachlorophane | not available | pHisoHex |
| hydrocortisone | Dioderm; Hydrocortisyl; etc. | Egocort; Cortef; Dermacort; etc. |
| hydroxyquinoline | Quinoderm* | not available |
| isotretinoin | Roaccutane | not available |
| keratolytics | Acnil; Medac; Clearasil; Dermaclear | Isophyl; pHorac; etc. |
| minocycline | Minocin | Minomycin |

# Great Britain   Australia

| Generic name | Trade Name | Trade Name |
|---|---|---|
| neomycin | Myciguent; etc. | Myciguent; etc. |
| oxytetracycline | Terramycin; Abbocin; Imperacin; etc. | Terramycin |
| polyethylene granules + benzalkonium chloride | } Ionax Scrub | Ionax Scrub |
| povidone-iodine | Betadine | Betadine; Povidone-K |
| retinoic acid = tretinoin | } Retin-A | Aberel; Airol; Retin-A |
| salicylic acid | Keralyt; an ingredient in many combination products | an ingredient of many combination products |
| selenium sulphide | Selsun; Lenium | Selsun |
| sulphamethoxy-pyridazine | } Lederkyn | Lederkyn |
| sulphur + resorcinol | Eskamel; Dome-Acne | Eskamel; pHorac |
| tetracycline | Achromycin; Tetrabid; etc. | Achromycin; Tetracyn; etc. |
| trimethoprim | Syraprim; Ipral; Trimopan | Triprim |
| trimethoprim + sulphamethoxazole | } Bactrim; Septrin | Bactrim; Septrin; Trib |
| aluminium oxide | Brasivol | Brasivol |
| zinc pyrithione | Head and Shoulders | not available |

| Generic Name | Trade Name | Trade Name |
|---|---|---|
| ampicillin | Penbritin; Amcill; Principen | Penbritin; Ampicin; etc. |
| benzoyl peroxide | Benoxyl; Panoxyl; etc. | Acetoxyl; Benoxyl; Panoxyl; etc. |
| chloramphenicol | Chloromycetin | Chloromycetin; etc. |
| chlortetracycline | Aureomycin | Aureomycin |
| clindamycin | Cleocin | Dalacin C |
| demeclocycline | Declomycin | Declomycin |
| erythromycin | Erythrocin; E-Mycin; etc. | Erythrocin; E-Mycin; etc. |
| hexachlorophene | pHisoHex | Hexaphenyl; pHisoHex |
| hydrocortisone | Dermacort; Cortril; Hydrocortone; etc. | Cortate; Cortef; Hyderm; etc. |
| isotretinoin | Accutane | not available |
| keratolytics | Keralyt | Keralyt |
| minocycline | Minocin | Minocin |
| neomycin | not available | Myciguent |
| oxytetracycline | Terramycin | Terramycin |
| polyethylene granules + benzalkonium chloride | Ionax Scrub | Ionax Scrub |
| povidone-iodine | Betadine | Betadine; Bridine; Proviodine |
| retinoic acid = tretinoin | Retin-A | Vitamin A acid Gel |
| salicylic acid | Keralyt; an ingredient in many combination products | Keralyt; Saligel |
| selenium sulfide | Selsun; Exsel | Selsun; Exsel |
| sulfur + resorcinol | Acne-Dome; Exzit | Acnomel; pHisoAc; Rezamid |
| tetracycline | Achromycin; Tetracyn; etc. | Achromycin; Tetracyn; etc. |
| trimethoprim | Proloprim; Trimpex | Proloprim |
| trimethoprim + sulfamethoxazole | Bactrim; Septra | Bactrim; Septra |
| aluminium oxide | Brasivol | Brasivol |
| zinc pyrithione | Head and Shoulders | Dan-Gard |

# ACKNOWLEDGEMENTS

The publishers are grateful to the following for permission to reproduce the photographs: A. G. E. Fotostock, Barcelona (pages 26, 40); Prof W. J. Cunliffe (page 88); the Department of Medical Illustration at the Welsh National School of Medicine (pages 13, 18, 21, 22, 24, 43, 62, 70, 74, 75, 79, 81, 82 and 83); Profs Gianotti and R. Caputo (page 77); Lederle Laboratories Ltd, Gosport (page 23); Picturepoint Ltd (pages 39, 42 and 76); and Wakewood Sunbeds (page 41).

The diagrams were drawn by David Gifford. The cover photograph was modelled by Sarah Godfrey, Ilona Ullman, Conrad Bauer, Adam Day and Gary Smith; the location shots on pages 27, 29, 30, 38, 47, 51 and 91 by Katharine Johnson and Gary Smith, at the Holiday Inn, Swiss Cottage, London, and on page 54 by Gary Smith and Stephen Banks; photography by Roland Kemp.

Finally, thanks are due to Jennifer Eaton, BSc, MSc, MPS, for information on British, North American and Australian drug name equivalents.

# INDEX

Page numbers in *italic* refer to illustrations.

camouflage sticks, 36
carbuncles, 85
children, infantile acne, 73
chloracne, 76; *77*
chlormycetin, 60
chlortetracycline, 63
chocolate, 33
cleanliness, skin, 35
cleansing creams, 35
Clearasil Cream Medication, 48
climate, acne and, 28, 94
clindamycin, 60, 65–6
clothing, acne and, 30–1, 37; *29*
collagen, 11
collars, 30–1, 37; *39*
colour, blackheads, 14
   skin, 10
comedolytic agents, 61
comedone naevus, 75; *75*
comedones, *see* blackheads
contraceptive pills, 31–2, 69, 70
cooking, 38
corticosteroids, 20, 61–2, 70–1
cortisone, 61
cosmetic acne, 25
cosmetics, 32, 36, 95; *30*
counselling, 24–5, 55
covering up spots, 32, 36; *38*
cryotherapy, 72
cyproterone acetate, 69
cystic acne, 78–80
cysts, 18; *15*
   cryotherapy, 72
   injection treatment, 62; *62*
   surgical treatment, 71

dandruff, 37
Debroxide, 57
demclocycline, 65
demethylchlortetracycline, 63
depression, 55, 95
dermabrasion, 72
Dermaclear, 48
dermis, 11; *9*
desquamation, 61

detergent lotions, 48
Diane, 69
diet, 11, 33, 44
Dioxin, 76
discos, 33, 38, 52; *40*
doctors, discussion with, 25, 55
   treatment by, 56–72, 95–6
drug treatment, 46, 56–71
   acne caused by, 77–8, 94
   local treatment, 57–62
   oral treatment, 63–71

eczema, 60, 84–5
elastin, 11
elderly people, acne in, 73–4
environment, acne and, 28, 37–8
   research, 90
Epanutin, 78
epidermis, description, 10; *9*
epilepsy treatment, acne and, 78
erythromycin, 60, 65, 83
Eskamel, 36
extractors, for blackheads, 45; *45*

family attitudes to acne, 52–3
fatty food, 33
fear of skin diseases, 50
fever, 79
folliculitis, 86
food, diet, 33, 44, 95
   preparation, 38; *39*
foundation creams, 32, 36
freezing treatment, 72
friends, advice from, 53–5
   attitudes to acne, 52
fringe acne, 25, 36

gels, 57
girls, as acne sufferers, 16, 28
grease, cosmetic acne, 25
   working with, 28, 31
greasy hair, 25, 31, 36
greasy skin, 11, 15–16
groin, acne of the, 80–2

oral treatment, 63–71
orange peel skin, 16
overalls, greasy, 31
oxytetracycline, 63

Panoxyl, 57
papules, 17; *15*
  mild acne, 20
  moderate acne, 21
papulopustules, 17, 21
parents, attitude of, 52–3
pastes, 57
peeling action drugs
  (keratolytics), 61
periods, menstrual, 31–2, 69
perioral dermatitis, 84; *83*
picker's acne, 23–5; *24*
picking spots, 23, 45, 93–4
pigmentation, blackheads, 14
  skin, 10
Pill, contraceptive, 31–2, 69, 70
pills, 63–71
plastic surgery, 19, 71–2
pock scars, 19
  surgical treatment, 71–2
pores, description, 10
  open, 16
povidone-iodine, 46
pregnancy, anti-androgen
  treatment and, 69–70
  tetracycline treatment and, 65
proprionebacterium acnes, 17
pseudomembranous colitis, 64,
  66
psoriasis, 37
pustules, 17–18
  squeezing, 45

Quinoderm, 58, 62

racial groups, acne and, 28, 90
rashes, tetracyclines and, 65
recreation, 38
research, 14, 87–92, 96
retinoic acid, 59, 66

Roaccutane, 66
rosacea, 20, 82–3; *82*

salicyclic acid, 61
scalp, acne of the, 80
scarring, 18, 19–20, 45, 93
  hypertrophic scars, 19, 20
  keloid scars, 19; *18*
  mild acne, 21
  moderate acne, 22
  pock scars, 19
  severe acne, 22
  surgical treatment, 71–2
  treatment, 19–20; *18*
scratching spots, 23, 45
sebaceous glands, 11, 12; *9*
  blackheads and, 15
  hormone treatment, 69
  seborrhoea and, 15–16
seborrhoea, 15–16, 35, 87–8; *13*
sebum secretion, 11, 15, 16, 33
  astringent lotions and, 36
  hormone treatment, 68–9
  research, 87; *88*
  ultraviolet light and, 40
  washing off, 35
Selsun, 37
senile comedones, 74
Septrin, 66
severe acne, 22; *23*
sex hormones, 16, 28, 50, 88, 94,
  95
sexual activity, 34, 95
shampoos, 37
shaving, 37
shaving rash, 37, 86
Simple Soap, 35
skin, cleanliness, 35
  colour, 10
  description, 10–11; *9*
  inflammation, 17
  redness, 20
  sunlight and, 39–44
sleep, lack of, 33
soap, 35

# Other books in the Positive Health Guide series

## ANXIETY AND DEPRESSION
*A practical guide to recovery*
**Prof Robert Priest**

We all get anxious and depressed at times, but for at least one person in ten these feelings are so overwhelming that they totally disrupt their lives. Prof Priest explains exactly what anxiety and depression are, what causes them, and what you can do to speed your own recovery – including relaxation and massage, ways of coping with difficult relationships, and when to seek medical advice.

## GET A BETTER NIGHT'S SLEEP
**Prof Ian Oswald and Dr Kirstine Adam**
For the millions of insomniacs, these world-renowned sleep experts help to break the vicious circle of anxiety over lost sleep leading to more restless nights. They offer practical, scientifically based advice on the best ways to avoid sleeplessness and wake refreshed each morning.

## THE HIGH-FIBRE COOKBOOK
*Recipes for Good Health*
**Pamela Westland**
**Introduction by Dr Denis Burkitt**
Although most people now realize the enormous importance of eating high-fibre food to help avoid many of the commonest Western ailments, few know how to put this knowledge into practice in a varied and interesting way. Here at last is a book that combines the healthy benefits of high-fibre eating with good imaginative home cooking.

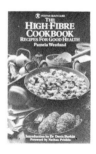

## THE BACK – RELIEF FROM PAIN
*Patterns of back pain – how to deal with and avoid them*
Dr Alan Stoddard

## BEAT HEART DISEASE!
*A cardiologist explains how you can help your heart and enjoy a healthier life*
Prof Risteard Mulcahy

## DON'T FORGET FIBRE IN YOUR DIET
*To help avoid many of our commonest diseases*
Dr Denis Burkitt

## ASTHMA AND HAY FEVER
*How to relieve wheezing and sneezing*
Dr Allan Knight

## OVERCOMING ARTHRITIS
*A guide to coping with stiff or aching joints*
Dr Frank Dudley Hart

## PSORIASIS
*A guide to one of the commonest skin diseases*
Prof Ronald Marks

## THE MENOPAUSE
*Coping with the change*
Dr Jean Coope

## DIABETES
*A practical new guide to healthy living*
Dr Jim Anderson

## HIGH BLOOD PRESSURE
*What it means for you, and how to control it*
Dr Eoin O'Brien and Prof Kevin O'Malley

## THE DIABETICS' DIET BOOK
*A new high-fibre eating programme*
Dr Jim Mann and the Oxford Dietetic Group

## STRESS AND RELAXATION
*Self-help ways to cope with stress and relieve nervous tension, ulcers, insomnia, migraine and high blood pressure*
Jane Madders

## VARICOSE VEINS
*How they are treated, and what you can do to help*
Prof Harold Ellis

## ECZEMA AND DERMATITIS
*How to cope with inflamed skin*
Prof Rona MacKie

## ENJOY SEX IN THE MIDDLE YEARS
Dr Christine Sandford

## CONQUERING PAIN
*How to overcome the discomfort of arthritis, backache, migraine, heart disease, childbirth, period pain and many other common conditions*
Dr Sampson Lipton